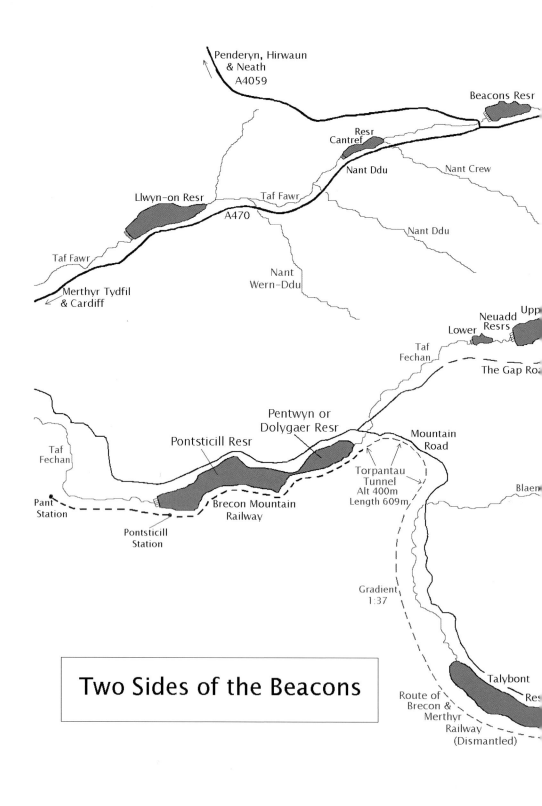

Two Sides of the Beacons

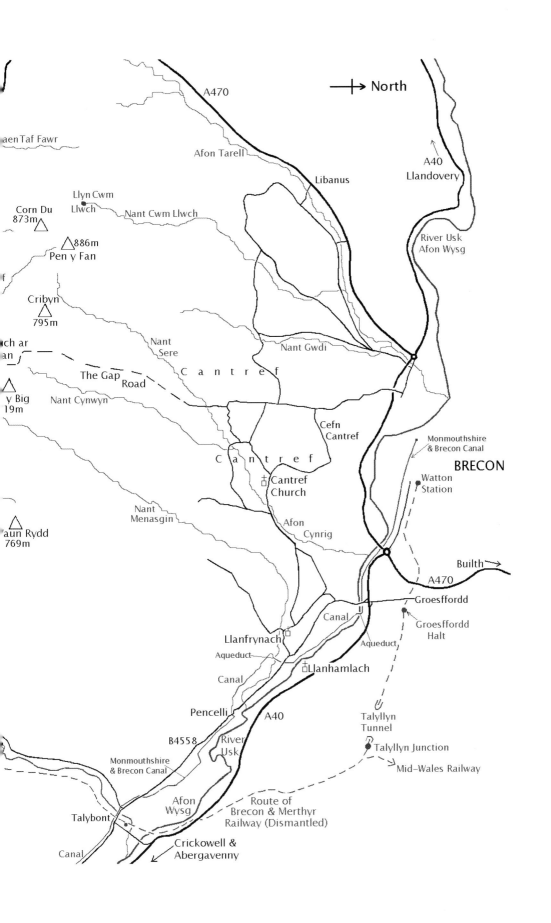

Old Cwmcynwyn

Standing amongst the ruins of Old Cwmcynwyn,
before the fireplace, cold and unsettled
by the bread-oven's open tomb;
where long ago children played,
tilling the warm ashes into tiny fields
planting the memories they would
carry when grown into a new world.
There they flourished on the level field they found
- but still in the dreams of old age,
to this hearth, on the hill, they were drawn.

Brychan Stephens
Cwmcynwyn

WHERE WE BELONG II
EIN CYNEFIN II

Life in the Beacons – Bywyd yn y Bannau
Then and Now   –   Ddoe a Heddiw

Golygydd/Editor
Susan Brook

Published by
Llanfrynach and Cantref Women's Institute
2011

First edition published in 2000

ISBN 978-0-9568375-0-9

Produced by Print Services Rhondda Cynon Taf CBC 2011

WHERE WE BELONG II
EIN CYNEFIN II

Life in the Beacons – Bywyd yn y Bannau
Then and Now   –   Ddoe a Heddiw

Profits from this book will go to local charities

So many people have helped in the production of this book it is impossible to name them all. From tea makers and cake bakers to historians and bookkeepers and most of all those who shared memories and lent photographs. The list is long.
To all of you - heartfelt thanks.

In particular my personal thanks to Eirwen Stephens, my invaluable helpmate in this extraordinary adventure, who, from the moment we met, always made me feel this is Where I Belong.

For bringing all the old photographs to life and for
IT support a big digital thank you to
Peter Casaru and Doug Varney of Say-Cheeze, Brecon.

Our much-loved local artist Meg Stevens gave permission for us to use two of her paintings on the cover:
"Brecon Beacons: Cow Parsley" on the front and "My Washing" on the back.

Meg, your work gives endless pleasure to so many. Thank you.

Susan Brook
& Llanfrynach and Cantref Women's Institute

Contents

William Phillips
Tŷ Fry Farm,
Llanfrynach 1971

I like to think that mine was a happy childhood, and having moved away from the area I cherish each opportunity to visit the farm to see family and friends, walk the dogs and revisit the places which give me such happy memories. It reminds me of where I come from and, more importantly.

Where I Belong
(from the first book)

Foreword

By Susan Brook

The first time I set eyes on the serried ranks of the members of Llanfrynach and Cantref Women's Institute, I knew I had met a force to be reckoned with. Here were women of hill-farming stock whose characters had been shaped by life in one of the most challenging landscapes in Britain.

I was right. My new companions were tough, stoical, sometimes unreadable, funny and very kind. How on earth would they receive this former journalist and TV presenter (Sue Jay) who had married a Welshman, Kim Brook, and come to live amongst them?

It was hard to see my skills as transferable to a rural WI. But in 2000 the members decided to mark the millennium by recording the story of life in the Brecon Beacons. Here was a job that, with their help and support, I could tackle. It was a pleasant surprise when the first edition of Where We Belong sold out. Ever since we have been pressed for more.

So here it is. Where We Belong II is a more complete history, with more stories from people who have witnessed a whole way of life in the Beacons change completely. Make no mistake; their memories are as vital a part of our history as the essential facts, figures and dates.

We describe life here today, including the devastation caused by the foot and mouth epidemic in 2001, and how this resilient community has come back even stronger.

Thank you to all those who have trusted us with precious memories. It has been a privilege to listen to you. Thank you to everyone who has loaned photographs.

This may not be the most academic of histories – but it is a very real reflection of the strength and vitality of the people who live their lives in the Brecon Beacons – Where We Belong.

Sue Brook, Cantref, April 2011

Cynefin – Belonging Plus

Photograph Garfield Kennedy

Cynefin

There are some words in every language that are so much part of the soul of the people that their full meaning can never quite be translated. In Welsh one of those words is "cynefin". It is used in the title of this book to mean "belonging" and it does. But Cynefin is belonging plus – it is belonging in the way a limb belongs to a body, part of how the whole body functions and is healthy.

Centuries of shepherding on the Brecon Beacons have created hefted flocks – sheep which know their part of the mountain and pass on that understanding to the next generation. Their territory – where they belong – is their cynefin.

Where We Began

Jon Pimm and Susan Brook

**"The difficulty of the terrain was as hard to overcome as
the bravery of the enemy."
Roman Governor Frontinus (AD 74-75)**

The Brecon Beacons form a dramatic landscape, with weather that can change from balmy and beautiful to life-threatening in minutes. A local guidebook describes them as "Hard on the legs, sharp on the senses, demanding on the body."

Look up at the serrated skyline formed by the Brecon Beacons and you can clearly make out the flat tops of Pen y Fan and Corn Du beside the mighty bastion of Cribyn and the tapered peak of Fan y Big, all formed more than 20,000 years ago as great glaciers of ice gouged their way through the landscape.

The mighty bastion of Cribyn

"Hard on the legs, sharp on the senses, demanding on the body."

Peaks and valleys were sculpted by the slowly moving glaciers, which diverted the River Usk into its present-day rocky gorge. Mounds of debris left behind form the landscape. Ty Mawr Pool, on the eastern side of Llanfrynach, was probably a kettle hole, formed by a huge pocket of ice melted from the glacier – a dramatic reminder of early climate change.

After the ice age, roaming tribes of hunter-gatherers gradually turned to farming and began to cultivate the area. A settled pattern of agricultural life continued largely unaltered for thousands of years.

Just as the ice age created the Brecon Beacons, so the Beacons themselves have in their turn, had a massive influence in creating a tenacious and resilient people.

Evidence of prehistoric settlement and land use can be seen in a number of places. There is a Neolithic-chambered tomb and Bronze Age standing stone near Llanhamlach. More recent evidence can be seen in the same area; further down towards Millbrook a Roman milestone with two early 4th Century inscriptions was found built into some old farm buildings, and in the wall of Llanfrynach Church there is a 10th Century sculpted stone.

The first farmers would have been Neolithic (New Stone Age) men, in about 4000 BC. They cleared large tracts of woodland and forests from the hills in order to grow crops and graze animals.

Later, it was the farmers who planted and laid the hedgerows, which are an important part of the landscape.

The Romans found Wales a "Tough nut to crack", according to the historian Tacitus, who wrote that when the Roman governor Frontinus (AD74-75) subdued the warlike tribe of the Silures (the British tribe settled in this area of Wales), he found that "The difficulty of the terrain was as hard to overcome as the bravery of the enemy."

Many families here can trace their history back generations, with knowledge of the landscape, the weather and most importantly their crops and animals, handed down from fathers and mothers to sons and daughters.

In the last century and a half there have been dramatic changes. The combustion engine, electricity, running water and of course television, mobile phones and the world wide web have been revolutionary – some think the changes they have brought about have been almost as cataclysmic as those wrought by the ice age itself.

In our second edition of Where We Belong, we have tried to honour this unique landscape and the generations who have farmed it.

To come alive, the telling of history must be more than a series of dates; conversely, to have relevance, anecdotes and memories need to be supported by facts. We have tried to combine both of these elements to reveal the flavour, atmosphere, character and history of the life in the Brecon Beacons – Then and Now.

Photograph Farmers Weekly

Jim Eckley shepherding on the Beacons c. 1973

Llanfrynach
From Roman Bath House to
Tŷ Bach Llanfrynach Loos

Llanfrynach isn't exactly 'on the road to nowhere' but the main routes of canal, train and road all just miss it. The main A40 by-passes the village by a mile. The nearest locks on the canal are either Pencelli or Brynich and the closest train stations were Groesffordd or Talyllyn. The absence of any major traffic route either going through or very near Llanfrynach has left the village with a very self-contained, unspoilt feel.

It has a great pub, an interesting church with the largest churchyard in Breconshire and Radnorshire, a village hall and about 300 residents.

The Romans, who always knew a good location when they saw it, settled here in grand style. The evidence points to Llanfrynach being the site of one of the wealthiest Roman civilian establishments known in central and northern Wales.

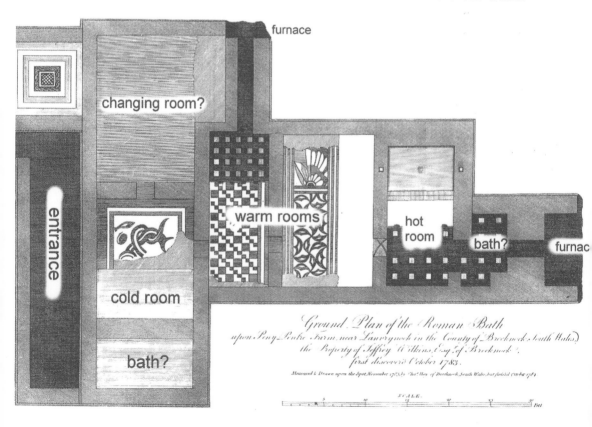

furnace

changing room?

entrance

warm rooms

hot room

bath?

furnac

cold room

bath?

Ground Plan of the Roman Bath upon Peny-Pentre Farm, near Lanvrynach in the County of Brecknock, South Wales. the Property of Jeffrey Wilkins, Esq. of Brecknock. first discovered October 1783.

Measured & Drawn upon the Spot, November 1783, by Thos Rees of Brecknock, South Wales, but finished October 1784

SCALE

Feet

It was probably a wealthy merchant or landowner of aristocratic descent who decided that Llanfrynach was the perfect place to build a luxurious bathhouse, the remains of which were discovered in 1783. Decorated with mosaics, it was 20m long with more than 12 rooms, under-floor heating (a hypocaust), a warm bath and two cold baths.

Obviously such a fantastic spa would have belonged to a magnificent villa. But that has never been found. It is more than likely that it lies beneath the present house of Maesderwen, just outside the village.

The first history of the Brecon Beacons was written by Thomas ap John of Llanfrynach. He died in 1616 and a very impressive monumental slab, which once lay on the floor in the chancel of Llanfrynach Church, described his lineage in the traditional Welsh way as: Thomas ap John ap Thomas ap John ap Rosser ap John ap Ieuan ap Philip ap Howell Gam. A drawing of the slab, by Hugh Thomas, is in the British Musuem.

Now Howell Gam was a paternal descendant of Brychan Lord of Brecknock, and also of Dafydd Gam, on whom Shakespeare modelled the character Fluellen in Henry V. Dafydd Gam's father, Llewellyn, Lord Penpont, died at Agincourt fighting for Henry V. The Gam family became known as the Games family and amongst other houses, they owned Tregaer Farm and Panney (Pannau). The Games family sold Tregaer to John Phillips, who was a founder member of the Brecknockshire Agricultural Society who died in 1763.

Tregaer

Mountain View 1904
Thomas Price (b. 1846, shoemaker), son Sidney (b. 1886),
Mr Dorey (chauffeur at Tŷ Mawr House), Mrs Oldacre? Annie Harris?

The picture of Llanfrynach that emerges from the census records is of a small but very close-knit community, probably the sort of place where people, 'knew their place'. Even today, some long-time residents remember when it was customary to doff a cap or curtsey to the gentry.

In 1970 Llanfrynach lost its Post Office, and in 1989 Llanfrynach School was closed. Those stories, and more about village life come later – including the one about how a gang of residents decided to revamp and run the village public conveniences.

Tŷ Bach Llanfrynach Loos may not provide quite the sybaritic experience offered by the Bath House, which once was the pride and joy of a previous Roman resident – but they are very convenient all the same. *(See more on p 159.)*

6

Cantref – Where Is It?

Trying to find Cantref can be a challenge. One has to forgive a newcomer, who has arrived right in the middle of it, for asking where it is!

SatNav is of questionable use in finding one of the scattered hill farms that make up Cantref, many of them up completely different narrow lanes and tracks but sharing the same postcode.

Remote and isolated are not words you'd necessarily choose to describe a close-knit community. But paradoxically Cantref is just that. The need for close co-operation in farming the hills, combined with extended families going back generations, has created a community culture that remains strong and confident enough to welcome and absorb newcomers who make the effort to join in.

At least three times a year, at Christmas, for Cantref Sports and again at Harvest about 100 Cantref residents, past and present, meet up. These are events attended by every generation. To witness a whole community, knowing each other and gathering together, is testimony to a resilient local culture born of centuries of shared work and shared experience.

Photograph Susan Brook

The Grand Finale of Cantref Sports – Throwing the Wellie

Only about 70 adults currently live in Cantref, though there is a good crop of young farmers growing up here. Many would like to remain in the community in which they were born, but strict enforcement of planning rules has largely prevented new buildings, restoration of old ruins and the conversion of old farm buildings for people to live in.

Planning guidelines favour conversions intended for commercial use, such as self-catering accommodation, rather than residential. This means that there can be problems for people who are retiring from farming, or young people who want to live apart from Mum and Dad, but within working distance of the farm. The older generation often moves to town to make room, commuting back to the farm to look after children and stock. And new young farmers can find it difficult to create a home – Where They Belong.

But Cantref has not always been such a quiet backwater. Until the late 1800s Cantref was a busy stop on a main road – The Gap Road.

The Gap Road

Controversy still surrounds the well-known 'Gap' or 'Roman' road, which crosses the Beacons between Cribyn and Fan y Big and then runs through Cantref and down the Old Road to Brecon. Did the Romans build it to connect their settlement at Y Gaer, West of Brecon, with the fort now within Merthyr Tydfil? Easy to believe they did when you see how it is driven in a straight line, through the mountains, cutting a "v" on the ridge below Cribyn.

But there is no doubt that the Gap Road was once a main route from Brecon to the south, used by drovers to walk sheep and cattle from farms to towns and cities where they would be fattened up and slaughtered. In the days when refrigeration was not even a word, this was the only way to get fresh meat to the tables.

Servicing the drovers and their stock was part of the business of the Beacons and Cantref was an important gathering place for sheep and cattle, despite the fact that there were more direct routes to England. Leslie Williams speculates that the drovers may have chosen the longer route to avoid the deeply unpopular tollgates on the major roads.

There is a wonderful clump of Scots pines just beyond the hill gate on the Gap Road above Cwmcynwyn, one of hundreds, even thousands, which were planted by the drovers to indicate somewhere they would be guaranteed a welcome and safe grazing.

A pony trek stopped by the Scots pines on the Gap Road

Photograph by permission of Llyfrygell Genedlaethol Cymru/ The National Library of Wales

Welsh Drovers c. 1885

The Drovers

With thanks to Abigail Kenvyn and Brecknock Museum & Art Gallery

As early as 1349 there is a record of twenty drovers taking four hundred head of cattle from Brecon to Essex. By the mid-eighteenth century it is estimated that 30,000 cattle and sheep were exported to England every year.

"Heiptrw Ho! Heiptrw Ho!" Though no-one seems to know what it means, this is said to have been the shout of the drovers, echoing for long distances over the Brecon Beacons to announce that a vast procession of cattle, oxen, pigs and geese was on its way.

Today we are used to seeing livestock moved about the country in huge transporters, two or three tiers high. For our ancestors however, it was a very different story. To get fresh Welsh meat to the cities of England, livestock was moved hundreds of miles on foot. The extraordinary breed of men responsible for 'droving' huge numbers of livestock to the meat markets and fairs of England was the Welsh drovers.

Imagine a huge herd, led by Welsh black cattle with wide horns, with hundreds of other animals following behind, all being herded by men and their dogs. Other travellers could be delayed for hours if they met up with this huge stream of slow moving animals. Farmers along the drovers' routes knew to lock up their own animals when they heard the drovers' shouts. If their livestock joined the herd, there was no way to get them back.

So who were the Welsh drovers? To our eyes they may have looked rough and ready, but in fact the master drover, who was in charge of the herd, had to be a man of utmost integrity. In order to obtain the necessary annual licence to trade livestock, drovers had to be at least 30 years of age, be married and own a property. The ability to negotiate deals in the English language would have been a major asset.

Being scrupulously honest and trustworthy was essential. Farmers entrusted their whole livelihood to the care of the drovers when they set off on their long journey.

The drovers were not only responsible for the livestock on the way to market, but with huge sums of money on the way home. They were also trusted with letters and legal documents and large amounts of money to take to London to pay rents owed to landlords and to carry out other financial transactions not related to the livestock trade.

News was another valuable commodity they carried, providing a much needed communication link between England and Wales. Drovers brought back news of events great and small to their small, isolated communities. It is thought that Wales learned of the Battle of Waterloo and the defeat of Napoleon through the drovers.

Providing services for the drovers and their animals was part of the business of the Beacons. A number of pubs and inns with names such as 'The Drovers Arms' are part of that legacy, providing rest and food for the men while the animals would be safely enclosed in the fields nearby.

Welsh black cattle were ideal for droving. They were hardy animals that survived well on the Welsh hills, and when they reached their final destination, they put on weight quickly before they were sold.

All the stock was the responsibility of the drover and being in charge of such large herds, often hundreds strong, took real skill. The animals had to be in top condition when they arrived at the markets so that they would fetch the best possible price. Drovers needed to ensure the animals had plenty of food and rest, while still keeping a pace of 15-20 miles a day to ensure they reached their destination on time.

The animals' health and welfare were paramount, and to protect their feet on these long journeys they were fitted with special shoes. This was a huge task. Unlike horses, cattle have cloven hooves and required two crescent shaped shoes per foot. This meant eight shoes were needed per beast, a time consuming job when there could be hundreds of cattle all needing to be shod.

The old farm in Cantref called Tir-Ciw is a reminder of those times. Tir means place and Ciw is an old Welsh word for the special kind of shoe put on cattle. So Tir Ciw is a place for cattle to be shod or re-shod.

Sheep, pigs and geese were also given special shoes on their long journeys. Geese were walked through a mixture of soft tar and sand, which gave their feet a protective coating. Little boots of wool with leather soles were made for the pigs. Welsh corgi dogs were used to herd the cattle, as they were quick and agile enough to keep the animals on the road, whilst being small enough to avoid being kicked.

Droving slowly died out with the coming of the railways and improved transport. It had been a part of rural life for hundreds of years. As well as transporting animals to the markets and fairs of England, the drovers played a vital role in forging an important economic and cultural link between Wales and the rest of the world.

The Banks

If the outward journey with hundreds of valuable cattle, sheep and pigs was potentially dangerous, then imagine how vulnerable the drovers were on the journey home, when they would be carrying all the profits from the sale of the stock.

Not surprising then that this growing trade with London and other cities led to a number of drovers' banks being established including Brecon Old Bank, in 1778. The Black Ox Bank in Llandovery, founded in 1799, had a black ox on its notes to symbolise its links with the drovers.

Providing banking for the drovers became a lucrative business for Walter and Geoffrey Wilkins, whose family name was later changed to de Winton. Branches of the de Winton family have made their home in Tŷ Mawr and Maesderwen Llanfrynach since the seventeenth century.

A family party outside Maesderwen. William de Winton (1823 –1907) is on the right. Seymour de Winton (with a beard) is behind the ladies

The Wilkins brothers were successful merchants with the East India Company in the mid-eighteenth century when they founded Wilkins Bank to serve not only the drovers but the iron and coal industries which were booming in the South Wales Valleys. They also financed the building of canals and railways.

In 1890 Wilkins bank, which by that time had branches all over South Wales, was sold to Lloyds – something which was obviously viewed as rather a way-out adventure by Howard Lloyd, who wrote in his journal in 1917, "This extension into South Wales was regarded by some of the Board as a leap in the dark, Wales being a terra incognita."

But it turned out to be a risk worth taking. According to Mr Lloyd: "The district of South Wales proved itself a fine and fruitful field for banking."

He described the de Wintons as: "Men of wealth and position, willing to relieve themselves of the cares and responsibilities of active business life, but under no other necessity of disposing of their very sound, well-managed, extensive and profitable bank."

William de Winton served Brecon as High Sheriff and Mayor and was involved in the restoration of Brecon Priory. His son Wilfred Seymour de Winton of Tŷ Mawr also became a director of the bank and gave a huge amount of money to the Church in Wales.

After the Church in Wales split from the Church of England in 1923 and became disestablished, Wilfred decided to leave his entire estate, including Tŷ Mawr, to the Church. The bequest helped the Church fulfil one of Wilfred's greatest desires, that the Priory in Brecon should become a Cathedral when the Diocese of St. David's was divided to create the Diocese of Swansea and Brecon, also in 1923. But his generous gift to the Church meant that eventually his descendants had to find the money in order to buy back Tŷ Mawr.

Buying The Farm

Historically a vast number of farmers in the Brecon Beacons did not own the land from which they earned their living. Their farms were 'tied', which meant they were owned by someone else to whom they paid rent. In the 1800s just 27% of residents in Llanfrynach owned their own homes and only 14% of farmers owned their farms.

The chance that a tenant farmer would ever have enough money to buy a farm has never been great. But sometimes a tenant did make enough money, by dint of hard work and good management, to make it possible. So when a tied farm came up for sale it was considered only fair that it was first offered to the tenant farmer.

Under instructions from the Right Hon. The LORD GLANUSK.

BRECONSHIRE.

PARISHES OF

Llanhamlach, Llanfihangel, Talyllyn, Llansaintffraid,
Llangasty-Talyllyn, Llangorse, Llanfrynach,
Llanveigan and Cathedine.

The Peterstone & Trebinshun
ESTATES

PLANS and PARTICULARS OF SALE
OF

Valuable Freehold Farms,
Licensed Premises,
Cottages and Gardens,
Small Holdings, Rent-Charges,
Etc.

WHICH WILL BE OFFERED FOR SALE BY AUCTION AT

THE CASTLE HOTEL, BRECON,

ON

FRIDAY, the 5th day of JULY, 1918,

At 1.30 o'clock in the Afternoon,

BY

Messrs. Stephenson & Alexander

(F.A.I.)

(D. T. ALEXANDER, J. A. ALEXANDER, H. G. ALEXANDER)

Plans, Particulars and Conditions of Sale may be obtained upon application to

Messrs. LEE & PEMBERTONS,
44, Lincoln Inn Fields,
LONDON,
W.C. 4

J. H. TURMEDGE,
Estate Office,
Glanusk Park,
CRICKHOWELL, Breconshire,

Or to the Auctioneers, 5, HIGH STREET, CARDIFF.

Not surprising then that there were a lot of disgruntled tenants in 1918 when Lord Glanusk put his Peterstone and Trebinshin estates up for sale. There was huge interest from neighbouring landlords, prospective landowners and of course the tenant farmers, many of whom were extremely angry at not being given first refusal and the chance to negotiate a deal privately.

At 1.30pm on 5th July 1919, the day of the sale, at the Castle Hotel in Brecon, the mood was at fever pitch, not least because one of the main bidders was the very rich, self-made David Morgan, founder of the department store, Morgans, The Hayes, Cardiff. He had already bought Pencelli Castle with the Lordship of Pencelli and Llanbrynean House and Farm in Llanfrynach and his stated ambition was to own all the land he could see from his window at Llanbrynean.

David Morgan and Llanbrynean

But David Morgan was no stranger to dire poverty and the struggle of the tenant farmer. His could be the plot of a popular novel. As young boy, aged 12, son of an industrious and tenacious woman who has fought for survival after seeing her family evicted from its hill farm, he left home, made his fortune and returned home as an old man to buy every farm he can see from his bedroom window.

David Morgan was a real Victorian: enterprising, religious and frugal. It was said of him that what made him rich was: "Not so much what he made, as what he saved", a characteristic common to many hill farmers, particularly those who experienced the terrible poverty that could be their lot in what became known as the 'Hungry forties'.

He was 'Victorian' by nature, and he also spent practically his whole life under her reign. His first memory was in 1837, when his father returned home from Brecon market, arriving on his pony at a trot instead of its customary walk.
He called to his wife Ann, "Mae'r Brenin wedi marw!" (The King is dead). King William IV had died, and Victoria was Queen.

For 23 years, the Morgan family had farmed Cae Crwn, Battle. After a long and bitter struggle to make ends meet they were evicted. Destitution and the prospect of becoming parish paupers stared them in the face. But a member of the Chapel at Pontfaen gave them shelter in an empty farmhouse and the family survived.

Ann Morgan was a hard taskmaster, even to her children. David Morgan was reported as saying: "If I had not been able to escape her often, I think she would have thrashed me within an inch of my life." David and his brothers were taught to read and write and rudimentary maths in a one-room school over the blacksmith's shop in the village of Cradoc.

In 1857 Ann Morgan heard that Llanbrynean Farm was vacant. Before the agent would let them be tenants he insisted on inspecting their home.

Ann was a compulsive worker, her home immaculate. She passed the test; the family moved in to their new farm of 141 acres and began to prosper.

David Morgan (1833 – 1919)

But David was not cut out to be a farmer. In exasperation at his ineptitude, Ann packed her son off, when he was twelve years old, to work for a relative in Rhymney who had a shop. There he earned his first wages of six shillings, of which he saved four.

When he was 14 he was apprenticed to a draper in Newport. He also worked for a while in a Dickensian shop in London where he slept under the counter, and later he almost decided to settle in Birmingham until his mother persuaded him to start a business nearer home.

His first successful store at Pontlottyn was just the beginning. Morgan went on to found Wales' premier department store, which closed in January 2005, after 125 years in business.

In 1874 he was able to buy the freehold of Llanbrynean, which his brother William continued to farm. They built a new farmhouse to replace the old. Owning Llanbrynean must have been his proudest achievement, until in 1918 Lord Glanusk put the Peterstone and Trebinshun estates up for sale.

At that packed and memorable auction, David Morgan achieved his dream. Seventy-three years after leaving home, he was now in a position to spend a lot of his hard-earned fortune on buying huge tracts of farmland and farms in the Usk Valley: the land he could see from his bedroom window.

Sale of
Peterstone Court and Trebinshin Estates
Castle Hotel, Brecon
5th July 1919

Pencelli Court	148 acres	£4,025	David Morgan
Tynewydd Farm	130 acres	£5,500	David Morgan
Dolymaes	314 acres	£5,000	David Morgan
Millbrook Farm	99 acres	£4,400	W D Smith
Highgrove	190 acres	£2,800	David Morgan
Greenways Slade	325 acres	£6,800	Powell Dyffryn
Brynllicci Farm	243 acres	£3,450	David Morgan
Manest Court	318 acres	£9,000	Bryn Morris (tenant)

At the sale of Manest to its tenant the whole assembly clapped in approval.

Auction of Tied Property
Bush Inn, Brecon
24th July 1802

This auction of property from Viscount Ashbrook's Estate also created huge interest.

Lot 1   All that capital Mansion House, messuages, farm lands with appurtencances, called Tregare, situate in the Parishes of Llanfrynach and Llanvigan and a House, Garden and Orchard in the village of Llanfrynach, containing together by estimation 367 acres in the occupation of the Representatives of Edward Morgan, deceased, and David Jones, under a lease for 21 years commencing from Michaelmas 1796 at the clear yearly rent of £100. Also Tir Hir 64 acres held by above at £42.10.0. yearly.

Lot II   Also Cwm Orgwm, otherwise Coed y Bedw 111 acres held as above at clear yearly rental of £27.10.0. (Wood of birches)
NB There is a rent charge of £8 annually issuing out of this farm, and payable to the poor of Llanhamlach, which the Tenant pays, and the farm will be sold subject to such Rent charge.

Lot III   Also, All those two messuages, farms and lands, with their appurtencances called Panney and Pen y Wain, containing together 204 acres in the occupation of John Parry, under a Lease for 21 years, which will expire at Michaelmas 1829, at the yearly rental £63.
Also all that messuage & lands called Cae Cradog, estimation 9 acres in the occupation of Thomas Aubrey, as Tenant at Will, at the yearly Rental of £5.5.0.

Lot IV   All that messuage, farm and lands called Tynllwyn, adjoining Panney Farm situate in the Parish of Llanfrynach aforesaid, containing 115 acres in the occupation of Thomas Watkins and William Jones under a Lease for 14 years commencing from Michaelmas 1796 at the clear yearly Rental of £52.10.0d.

Lot V   All that rough Piece or Parcel of pasture ground called Coed Cae Janet, situate in the Parish of Llanfrynach aforesaid, containing 23 acres, now held by William Mosely at the clear yearly rent of £2.2.0d.

The above farms have an unlimited Right of Common for all manner of Cattle on the adjacent Commons and the several houses and out-houses have been lately put in complete repair at very considerable expense..

Mr. Jeffreys Wilkins of the Priory bought several farms, but not Cwm Orgwm.

Eliza Davies
1847 – 1922

20

Eliza Davies – A Woman Alone

Life in a rural community during the nineteenth century was life without a safety net; there was no welfare state to catch the sick or the needy. Women worked as ordinary field labourers and children were frequently called on to swell the workforce.

If one image could sum up just how hard life could be for a woman in rural Wales at the end of the eighteen hundreds, it is that of Eliza Davies (1847-1922). Eliza had eight children. The first, David, was eleven years old when he died in 1881. Her husband died in 1892, leaving her with six more children and pregnant with a baby girl. Alone, she had to cope with the farm and the children, so it was hardly surprising that the new baby died the day after she was born in 1893.

In those days it was not the practice for women to hold farm tenancies She and her young family were asked to leave. She had no state help and no one to turn to. Many years later, one of her sons, Richard (Dick) Davies of Tyle Llwyd, described her struggle. He said there was no help for the family except what they could find for themselves. Survival was only possible by Eliza going out to work on local farms. She took her children to live at a smallholding near Libanus, which provided a meagre living for Eliza, who owned just a couple of cows and a heifer. Dick recalled long winter nights when his mother, worn out with toiling on a nearby farm, would return home, only to carry on working far into the night. Her granddaughter, Nancy Felton, says that although Eliza's husband could only make his mark, Eliza could read and write, and she paid a penny a week for the children to go to Libanus school. But as each child became 12 years old, he or she would leave home to find work to help those who were left behind.

In 1897 Eliza bought the first ton of slag to arrive in the Libanus district. Slag is a waste product from the iron industry, which was growing dramatically at that time. Ground to a fine powder, it was used along with lime and manure as a fertiliser. The farmers didn't think it would be much good. Eliza was probably driven to try it on her land because her two cows did not provide her with enough manure. The next year her grass was wonderfully green, and eventually slag became commonly used. The smallholding was then known as Caehaearn (iron field), possibly a name acquired as a result of Eliza's efforts. Today, it is familiar to thousands of tourists, as it is the site of the National Park Visitor Centre.

In 1906 Eliza moved to Tyle Llwyd on the de Winton estate in Cantref, where she died, and where two of her sons, Dick and Dai, continued to farm until the mid-1950s.

There is a splendid photograph of her in her widow's weeds on page 90.

Richard Davies (Dick Tyle Llwyd)
(1889 – 1969)
Served as an ostler in the Royal Army
Service Corps, breaking in horses and
driving a team of six
(His story is on p 63)

Photograph taken at Clark's Photographic Studio
Private Price Phillips (1893 – 1979)
Montgomeryshire Yeomanry
(More about what happened to him as a farmer
on pages 76/7)

World War One

Wartime presented many farming families with one of the cruellest of choices – which son should stay on the farm and which should go and fight.

During both the First and Second World Wars, farming was a reserved occupation. The production of food was of national importance, so it was essential that some men remained at home to farm. Government officials kept a close watch on farms where there were several men of conscription age, to ensure that the right numbers were called up.

Eliza Davies' son Dick Tyle Llwyd and Price Phillips Caerau both made the most of their expertise and love of horses during the First World War. Dick and Price both joined cavalry regiments and Price saw service in France.

Happily both young men returned to the Brecon Beacons and went on to spend their lives farming here.

Sadly many others were not so fortunate. Each year the names of the local men who gave their lives in those wars and others are read in a Remembrance Service at one of the three churches of the Beacons Benefice and the words of the poet Laurence Binyon are quoted:

> They shall not grow old, as we that are left grow old.
> Age shall not weary them, nor the years condemn.
> At the going down of the sun and in the morning
> We will remember them.

Laurence Binyon's grandson, Edmund Gray, bought Crofftau, Cantref in the 1960s. He and his friends and family enjoyed it for many years until he sold it to Sue and Kim Brook. He is still a regular visitor to Crofftau and a lover of the Brecon Beacons.

After the war, Price Phillips married and eventually went to live in the tiny house in Cantref attached to the Nonconformist Chapel, Capel Twyn. These were the days when people would travel for miles to Chapel on Sundays. at least once and often twice. Capel Twyn was famous for years for its annual sports day with legendary country teas.

Price Phillips' daughter Barbara, born in Capel Twyn in 1929, remembers her father as a very quiet man. "I wish now I had listened more to the stories he told about the war."

Village Life

Like many villages in the Brecon Beacons, Llanfrynach used to be largely self-sufficient. The census returns from 1841 to 1891 reveal blacksmiths, carpenters, coopers, dressmakers, tailors, shoemakers or cordwainers (there were 16 of those!), millers, grocers, publicans and butchers, all making a living.

Most of what the villagers needed they either grew or made themselves. The streets would have been busy with tradesmen, people going to and from work and to the post office, pub or school. Villagers could shop in at least one and sometimes two grocery shops and for a while there were one or two local butchers. There were two public houses, the White Swan and the Victoria Inn.

In a study of the census records of 1841 – 1881, Carol Webb, former resident of The Forge, Cantref, drew a picture of Llanfrynach as a small but very close-knit community, most of whose needs were met locally.

"In fact Llanfrynach had similar facilities to nearby Brecon, except for commercial organisations such as banks. However, such institutions were probably unnecessary, because most of the time goods and services were probably bartered. And even if money did change hands it would probably have been circulated within the community, from labourer to tradesman, from tradesman to farmer and back to labourer again.

"Many occupations were organised on a family basis – from the labourer who would be joined in the fields by his wife and children at busy times such as harvest, to the blacksmith who trained his sons to continue the business and even to the de Wintons whose family were by tradition magistrates, bankers and Borough Councillors."

The Milk Round

One sight familiar to village residents until the mid 1950s was that of Leslie Williams delivering milk from Abercynrig. After the cows were milked he took the milk in churns straight to people's doors, measuring it out with a pint measure.

Leslie remembers regularly stopping to talk to women who had to walk to the various taps in the village for water. The water supply for Llanfrynach came from a spring on the left hand side of Tregaer Road, just before the entrance to Tregaer.

The supply was piped to several sites in the village including Mountain View, Victoria Square, Tŷ Mawr Road (between the Post Office and the White Swan), Tŷ Fry Farm, School Row and at the side of Mizpah Chapel.

The taps were specially designed to conserve water. You had to press the tap down to make it flow and when you took your hand off the tap shut. This all worked well until the whole of Llanfrynach was put on the mains in 1953/4.

Leslie Williams and Anne Marie Lloyd leaving Abercynrig
with fresh milk in churns to deliver to houses in Llanfrynach.
1950

Older residents miss the days when the streets were busy with people going to and from their work, to get water, to shop at the Post Office or go to school. It all provided an instant social network on the village streets. And the pace of life was said to be slower, with people taking time to chat.

Ted Jones' (on right), born in Swan Cottage in 1895, chats with Roger Jones, a farmhand at Tŷ Fry. Ted's daughter, Barbara Harris, still lives in the village

The Post Office

Alice Jones was born in Llanfrynach in 1890. When she was fourteen, she began work at Llanfrynach Post Office. She learned Morse code, which she used to tap out and receive telegraph messages for the community. At the turn of the century the first telephones arrived in the village, and a small exchange was set up in the front room of her cottage in Church Row.

This tiny room became a Telegraph Office, Savings Bank, Telephone Exchange and Post Office. Alice had three children, Boyo, Margaret and Libby. Libby remembered the big square board on the wall, which was the exchange: "It had plugs in it attached to cords you would pull up and plug in to connect the different callers on the

26

Llanfrynach Exchange. There was a big bell attached to one of the oak beams in the ceiling, and Libby said it was so loud she thought the whole village could hear it ringing."

To connect anyone with an exchange outside Llanfrynach, Alice had to call the Brecon Exchange to make the onward connection and put them through. All the ringing was done manually, with a handle attached to the phone. During the Second World War, Alice was on call twenty-four hours a day. She slept on a sofa downstairs, so that when the GPO rang in the middle of the night to test that the line was working, she could answer the 'phone immediately Batteries kept in a shed outside powered the exchange and a man came every day to test them.

**Alice Jones in front of Llanfrynach Post office
with one of her daughters, Margaret**

Jean Phillips says it was 1938 when the first telephone was installed at her home, Upper Cantref. At the time there were 22 subscribers on the Llanfrynach exchange. If you were lucky enough to have a telephone in your house, all you had to do was pick up the receiver and Alice would ask you what number you wanted.

The New Houses

Denise Balding (née Naylor) was born in 1948 in Bridge Row – a small row of houses, which used to stand by the bridge in Llanfrynach. As a small child she remembers her mother getting water for washing in a bucket out of the river, the Nant Menasgin. Their drinking water came from the tap in the wall in Victoria Square.

When Denise was about five years old, the family was allocated one of the new council houses in Waunberllan. The move from one end of the village to the other seemed huge: "How will I find my way home after school?" she asked her Mum. "You'll see my blue curtains in the window," was the reassuring reply.

The Council Houses in Waunberllan, built in 1944, now all privately owned

There were lots of children to play with. Denise was the second oldest of seven and she remembers seven or eight children in the Pugh family, and the Watkins family with eleven children.

For fun they played hide-and-seek in the village, and loved dare games, running over the fields in the dark. There were crab-apple fights round the 'bus shelter with crab-apples scrumped from Tŷ Fry orchard. Denise says: "It doesn't sound like a very interesting life, but we had some fun. We always felt very safe. We played and climbed trees in the churchyard or wherever we wanted.

Penny Wright rides Nino
Victoria Square, Llanfrynach, 1970

When Elizabeth Daniel and her daughters Tamsin and Rachel arrived in 1972 to live in Mountain View, they soon settled into village life. (See Elizabeth's story on p155).

Elizabeth recalled, "I loved going to the White Swan and have happy memories of the Phillips brothers from Cantref all singing in the bar. And over the road in the churchyard, once a year, a whole gang of local men would gather to scythe the grass and drink cider.

"Llanfrynach was a good community with other mums all taking our children to Llanfrynach School together. The school was a very unifying thing."

School

Tŷ Fry Farm, built in the seventeenth century
The first village school was in a room at the top of the stairs on the right

Tŷ Fry was the site of the very first school in Llanfrynach. The children would have walked up the stone stairs on the right to get to the classroom. In 1853 a new school was built on land given by the de Winton family.

Llanfrynach school log-book has numerous entries explaining why large numbers of children were absent – planting or picking potatoes, gardening, or looking after younger siblings to release the mother to work in the fields.

The school was a central part of community life until pupil numbers dropped dramatically and the governors were faced with the tough decision to close it. The Revd Peter Sims, who was chairman of the governors said, "One teacher could not manage the whole school, but we could not afford, and the council would not pay for, an extra teacher. We had to put the children's education first so the decision was made to close Llanfrynach School in 1989.

"Events at the school, such as plays and sports days, were events attended by the whole community. When they stopped, village life seemed to dissipate."

The oldest known photograph of Llanfrynach School, opened in 1853

Llanfrynach Primary School 1980
Back: Mrs. Margaret Merrick, Gareth Hope, Tom Bowcher, Isambard Nelson, Sean Hope, Miss Katherine Perkins.
Middle, Dean Naylor, Peter Rigsby, Steph Hopkins, Gillian Boxhall, Julie Eckley, Robert Davies, Michael Austin.
Front: Tamsin Daniel, Sally Hopkins, Carol Eckley, Fiona Austin, Rachel Daniel, Catie Hope, Ruth Bowcher.

31

Abercynrig

Abercynrig must be one of the oldest houses in the area, with its origins in the thirteenth or fourteenth century. It was owned by Dr William Awbrey, born in Cantref in 1529, a man who became one of the great movers and shakers of his era.

Dr William Awbrey 1529 –1595
Born in Cantref, lived in Llanfrynach

Dr Awbrey had a distinguished legal career; it was said that he was partly responsible for saving the life of Mary Queen of Scots at her trial. He also took a leading part in the suppression of piracy. All this made him a rich man. When he died in 1595, he was buried in the old St Paul's Cathedral and was said to be worth £2,500 a year – a fortune in those days. He owned property all over Breconshire.

The next family to make a huge contribution to the history of Abercynrig was the Jeffreys. In the middle of the seventeenth century, Colonel Jonathan Jeffreys bought Abercynrig from the profits of his trade as a mercer, a dealer in high-class textiles. In his book about Abercynrig, Revd J Jones-Davies writes about mercers that, "The very word savours of luxury and opulence."

An Irish family called Flowers, one of whom became Viscount Ashbrook, followed the Jeffreys family and he in turn sold it to Captain John Lloyd in 1800.

The Lloyd family, then living at Dinas, Llanwrtyd, was financially in a bad way when John, the eldest of eight children, left in 1764 at the age of 16, to join a ship serving the East India Company.

His first, very lowly, job was as a surgeon's servant. During thirty years of service he was steadily promoted, paid off his family's debts and finally made two very lucrative voyages as a Captain of an 800-ton East Indiaman.

Captain John Lloyd, 1748 – 1818

After an adventurous career during which he was shipwrecked, involved in a major battle at sea, was wounded and spent two years in prison in Bangalore, he returned to Brecknock where in 1800 he bought the Abercynrig Estate of 745 acres. Abercynrig has been in the ownership of the Lloyd family ever since.

But it was Sir John Lloyd, who died in 1954, who was the first member of the family to make Abercynrig his home. He was followed by Major William Rhys (Bill) Lloyd, and in 2003 Richard Lloyd and his wife Mary moved to Abercynrig and undertook a major restoration of both the house and the garden.

Abercynrig

Setting off to deliver the milk from Abercynrig
Richard Lloyd in the driving seat and Ivor Williams, Abercynrig Mill, beside him

Vanished – the Hamlet of Felindre

Vanished – Bridge Cottages at Felindre – opposite Abercynrig Mill
Leslie Williams' mother is in the pony and trap

While Llanfrynach has changed dramatically and is still a thriving village, its neighbour for hundreds of years, the hamlet of Felindre has all but vanished.

In his history of Breconshire Hugh Thomas (1673 – 1720) says, "There are two villages, Llanfrynach and Velindre and about 60 families in the whole parish." The fact that this community warranted a post box in Victorian times illustrates a good number of people living in Felindre then.

Leslie Williams was born in 1919 and has lived in Abercynrig Mill all his life. But the view that Leslie remembers from his childhood has completely vanished, along with a bustling community, with more than enough children to form a couple of football teams.

From his home in the Mill, Leslie and his wife Joyce look across the Cynrig to an empty field where once there were two groups of cottages, home to several families. Leslie remembers the names of all the householders; "There were large families of Evans's, Williams's and Jones's as well as families called Price, Powell and Meredith.

"John Jones' wife used to get her water out of the river Cynrig and sometimes our gander would hiss and chase her from the river. As a small boy, she would give me a penny to swear at the gander to drive him away. We never grumbled that there was nothing to do, for we organised our own games, hare-and-hounds, paper-chase, hide-and-seek etc. In winter we used to sledge down on the snow in Cae Shon Walter.

"We were able to form two football teams and as they grew older the best of them were picked to play in the Llanfrynach Football Club. The field known as Cae Shon Richard just became known as the Football Field. The Club gradually attracted players from Brecon and beyond. There were no posh changing rooms and they bathed in a couple of zinc baths and hot water from the copper boiler.

Trefedw – cottages in the field beyond Bridge Cottages. Also vanished.

"Between the World Wars no less than seven cottages vanished or became ruins. Beyond Bridge Cottages were another two cottages called Trefedw, although some called them Tre Bedw. Bessie Evans who worked at Dinas as a nanny lived at Trefedw before moving to Dinas Lodge in Brecon, where she lived for 40 years until her death in 1994.

"The last people to live in Trefedw were Bill Griffiths, a carpenter who had a business in Brecon and his wife Mag, who was the daughter of Aythan Powell who had been bailiff of Berllan Farm, the home farm of Dinas. When he retired they moved to Brynygarn which we all called the Round House and whose ruins you can still see today. Other tenants of Brynygarn were Fred Powell the champion hedger and after that the Watkins family."

Cefn Cantref

Altitude counts for a lot in the Brecon Beacons; Cefn Cantref is only a short distance from Felindre and Abercynrig, but at 300 metres (1,000 feet) above sea level, Cefn Cantref is 'an overcoat cooler'. It is a stunning location, with views of the Brecon Beacons that have long been a magnet for artists and photographers.

Once the whole of Cefn Cantref was one huge farm with a grand old farmhouse and large stone barns. In 1881 the Watkins family took over the farm.

The Old Farmhouse at Cefn Cantref
Outside are Howell Watkins' brothers and sisters

Howell and Ann Watkins had 17 children, one of whom, Ivor Watkins, went on to farm neighbouring Bailyhelig. Their granddaughter Marion Davies, who today lives in Cradoc, says the photograph was taken after the birth of their tenth child, the first to be born after their move to Cefn Cantref in 1881.

Howell and Anne Watkins
Cefn Cantref Farm 1881

The farm was part of the Ffrwdgrech Estate until 1927 when it was sold, along with Gaer Farm, Cradoc, to the tenant, Edmund Jones. In 1935 he decided to move to the Gaer and sold the land to Brecon Council, which divided it up into smaller parcels and built homes on them. The idea was to create smallholdings for rent to young farmers to give them a start in a farming career.

Elma Higgins and her husband Ivor took on one of the Smallholdings of about 11 acres in 1963. It was the Christmas Eve after they moved to their new home that Ivor Higgins looked over the fields to the old farmhouse and saw flames shooting into the sky.

The nearest telephone kiosk was at Pontbrengarreg (which everyone calls Pontbren) and was often out of order. Ivor ran to his neighbour, they leapt into a car, and drove to Brecon police station to raise the alarm. Meanwhile the owners of Cefn Cantref, Mel Williams, his mother and uncle, were enjoying a Christmas Eve drink in Brecon. The first they knew was at 11pm when someone came to the pub and told them their home was on fire.

Mel said: "There was a big oak beam over the chimney breast which must have caught fire. It was a windy night and there was a lot of old timber in the building. The fire would have caught hold very fast. The old house was three storeys high, with more than 20 rooms in it. By the time the fire brigade got there it was well and truly alight. The ice on the pond was ten inches thick and they had to break through it to get the water. There was no chance of saving the house. Within an hour or so it was gone, along with everything we owned. It was terrible."

A new modern home was built for Mel just eight feet away from the old foundations. He said it didn't have the bumps, bangs and squeaks of the old house. And there was a species of mouse, "A big brown chap" that he has never seen since the fire either.

Mel died in 2008 and neighbours Veronica Sullivan and John Wiggins bought the house. It was their ambition to demolish it and build a replica of the original farmhouse that had been destroyed. After a huge amount of research into the history and appearance of the old farm, and initial encouragement by the Brecon Beacons National Park Authority, the couple was bitterly frustrated and disappointed to be refused planning permission for their project.

The wonderful old barns that had been part of the original farm and had survived the fire had become part of Brian Williams' dairy farm *(to find out about what happened to that see p 131)*. Now, after another long planning battle, the barns are being converted into homes by Bwydd Developments. These are the thoughts of the owner, Tim Organ:

"When Howell and Annie Watkins lived at Cantref, there is no doubt that there were many more people living and working off the land than now. Now that farming has changed in every respect the great stone barns at Cefn Cantref lack the flexibility and construction qualities to be efficient agricultural buildings. They are, however, ideal for recycling into sustainable and invigorating homes.

"They have much greater space than can ever be economically created in new homes. The stone, slate and timber give a powerful sense of permanence which, coupled with new green technology, can be the ideal components for innovative and comfortable dwellings.

"Cefn Cantref is a very special place from which to explore, appreciate and respect the mountains and the wildlife. The local pond offers a place for relaxation and enjoyment for those who come to live in the barns and the community at large. We are optimistic that people who appreciate the pleasures and qualities of Cefn Cantref will make a positive contribution to the local community.

We remember the first time we met with the local community of Llanfrynach in the Village Hall. It is fair to say that we were greeted with suspicion, and not a little hostility. However, a great deal has happened since then. The caution has evaporated and friendships have been established. We want to respect the history of the buildings and place, and to be a positive addition to the fabric of the community."

Photograph Ivor Jay

The Pond at Cefn Cantref – home to the Great Crested Newt

Two Sides of the Beacons

In spite of the challenges presented by vast tracts of empty moorland, the ties between farming communities on both sides of the high peaks of the Brecon Beacons have always been strong. Common grazing of unfenced pasture, which includes not only the North side of the Beacons, but also the upper parts of the valleys of the Taf Fechan and the Taf Fawr on the South side, has always required farmers to co-operate when the sheep are gathered.

But it was not only the farmers who had business on the hills. Both the Church and Brecknock Rural District Council included communities on both sides of the Beacons within the boundaries of Cantref.

William (Bill) Phillips, collected rates on horseback

The challenge of collecting the council rates from this sparsely populated area fell to William (Bill) Phillips. He traveled on horseback from his home at Pontbren Farm, Cantref to remote farms and small communities in the farthest corners of the District of Cantref. He rode to Nant Ddu in the valley of the Taf Fawr, and in the far West, the area of the Hepste, on the outskirts of Penderyn, all considered as part of Cantref.

While the hill farmers were dealing with one sort of flock, the Rector of Cantref had to face the challenge that his flock inhabited the largest parish in England and Wales, which also spanned both sides of the Beacons. He had the care of congregations and Churches in Cantref and Nant Ddu and undertook (or more likely his poor curate undertook) a similar journey to the one made by Bill Phillips.

Theophilus Jones, in his History of Brecknockshire, sympathises with the Rector because he was only paid forty shillings a year for this "Tedious ride and extraordinary duty". In 1923 the parish boundaries were redrawn, but the peak of Pen y Fan still lies in the parish of Cantref.

If you travel southwards over the Beacons by the Gap Road, you descend towards Merthyr Tydfil through the valley of the Taf Fechan. This is where the Richards family had made its home for more than 300 years. The first family record is of Howell ap Richards, born at Coed Hir in 1697. The family farmed at Abercriban and made the name famous as one of the most respected and successful Welsh Mountain Pony studs in the world.

Mr Llewellyn Richards (1822 – 1902) and Mrs Gwenllian Richards of Coed Hir, Taf Fechan, 1850s.

In his 70s Howell William Richards, born in 1845, wrote a journal about his life in the Taf Fechan Valley and Abercriban Farm. These are a few extracts:

"The Taf Fechan Valley is about the highest valley in Wales; the bottom end is over 1000 ft, bad for corn growing but good for wintering cattle – always came out better than when put in. The hay harvest was pretty hard for the women because we had to mow it all with a scythe. The mowing machine was the first good implement in the haymaking.

"When I was brought up... there was only one candle lit at the same time for the whole house, which was made out of sheep fat. As my mother was a good hand I think she used to make short ones for the barn lantern to take out to the stable. The first oil lamp I saw was in the year 1873 at my home."

But life in this secluded valley, which had been much the same for centuries, was to change dramatically, victim to a very thirsty industrial revolution.

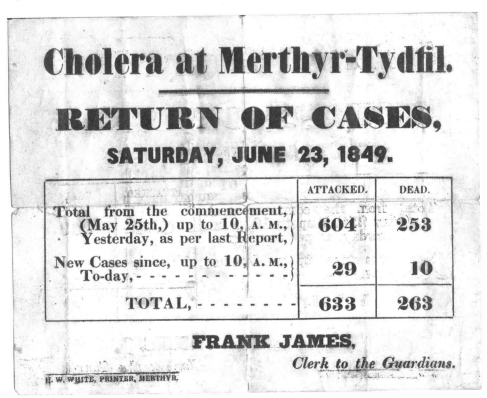

Cholera at Merthyr-Tydfil.

RETURN OF CASES,

SATURDAY, JUNE 23, 1849.

	ATTACKED.	DEAD.
Total from the commencement, (May 25th,) up to 10, A. M., Yesterday, as per last Report,	604	253
New Cases since, up to 10, A. M., To-day, - - - - - - - - - -	29	10
TOTAL, - - - - - - - -	633	263

FRANK JAMES,
Clerk to the Guardians.

H. W. WHITE, PRINTER, MERTHYR.

In Merthyr Tydfil 'the King of Terrors', cholera, struck three times, in 1832, 1849 and 1866. The town was cleansed with disinfectant and lime but hundreds of people died as the virulent water-borne disease flourished in the absence of a clean fresh water supply.

By the mid 1800s the rapidly expanding industries and burgeoning population in the South Wales Valleys and Cardiff needed water in vast quantities. Until then Cardiff had been little more than a large village or small town, and had no access to sufficient fresh water needed by the influx of thousands more people.

It was a challenge to which the Victorian engineers came up with a bold solution: they proposed flooding some of the valleys in the Brecon Beacons, creating reservoirs from which water could be piped into Merthyr, the South Wales Valleys and Cardiff.

Merthyr & District Urban Council decided to build a series of reservoirs on the headwaters of the Taf Fechan on the south side of the Beacons, just below Bwlch-y-Groes on the Gap Road. They were to become Upper and Lower Neuadd, Dolygaer (later called Pentwyn), and Pontsticill Reservoirs.

For the hard-hit citizens of the Valleys they were to be a godsend; but flooding the Taf Fechan Valley was to hit the Richards family of Abercriban Farm hard. They, and many others, had to leave their farms, homes to many generations of their families and with acres of good hill grazing, to be flooded.

This was a difficult time for Howell Richards:

"What I know about sheep and what I do not know.

"I had to manage a flock of 1000 sheep when I was seventeen – then I found out how little I knew.

"When I took over Blaentaf and Pendola farms of Mr John Williams in the year 1910 he had 9 hundred wether and 5 hundred ewes and 250 lambs. The big number of wethers improved the appearance of the flock and much better to stand hard winters.

"The reason I took the farms over was because Abercriban was taken over for making a reservoir and I had three restless sons about leaving school who thought they knew a lot about sheep. A boy in his teens with pony and dog will do more hill work on certain days than a grown up, but football matches must not be missed. The boys were in Cefn Coed School as dayboys with train very convenient.

"I had them at 5 o'clock and Saturdays and Sundays all day. So I did all the shepherding with them. But after they left school they were not long before they joined up (to fight in World War I).

Between the two oldest boys and their sister they were away 9 years between them and left me by myself for three years only with Willie when home from school. By then I had about 6 farms or pieces of them as they were broken up by the reservoir making.

"The Taf Fechan Valley has four reservoirs: the first Dolygaer was made in the year 1860 before the Brecon and Merthyr (railway) *which meant a lot of horse work. The Upper Neuadd in 1879 made all with pick and shovel. Then Lower Neuadd in 1893. Pontsticill was made in 1911 but not complete until 1920. They had to stop work during the war years. But took Aberciban House where I was living and all the low lying land and I had to make a move."*

Abercriban Farm – Home of the Richards family for more than 300 years

The Richards family moved to a new home in Brynhyfryd in Talybont-on-Usk, and their rambling old farmhouse disappeared under the floodwaters, which also engulfed the little church at Taf Fechan, where the family had worshiped.

Commoners from Cantref and Llanfrynach, who had grazing rights on the 64 acres of land that became the Neuadd Reservoirs, were paid compensation. In a public meeting, held in the White Swan Public House on 13th May 1904, they decided to spend the money on the Parish Hall, now called Cantref and Llanfrynach Community Hall and still very much at the heart of local life.

Taf Fechan Valley before being flooded to make the Pontsticill Reservoir
Abercriban Farm is right in the centre of the photograph

After the flood – the Pontsticill Reservoir

Photograph courtesy of Glamorgan County Record Office

Building Cantref No 2 Reservoir at Nant Ddu, 1884 – 1892

Cardiff Council instigated the Taf Fawr Scheme, which was to quadruple the city's supply of water, and which created the huge reservoirs one can see today driving on the A470 from Brecon to Merthyr Tyfil.

A temporary township of labourers and engineers arrived to carry out the work. Though there are only twelve houses in the small hamlet of Nant Ddu, the 1891 census shows a staggering labour force of 310 people living there. Thirty-two huts each housed up to ten or twelve people. They came from all over Britain, from Bloxwich to Bournemouth. Most of them listed their occupation as 'Navvy'.

The first reservoir to open was Cantref Reservoir (known at the time as Cantref No. 2) in 1892, followed by the Beacons Reservoir in 1897 and the Llwyn-on in 1902. The whole scheme cost £380,000. Today most of the work of those engineers and navvies is hidden under 1220 million gallons of water that fill the three reservoirs which are such outstanding landmarks.

From Shared Work to Making a Profit

It took one of Cantref's oldest residents, Ivor Phillips of Tylebrythos, born in 1908, to highlight one of the major differences between life now and at the turn of the century.

Asked by Eirwen Stephens what he thought had been the biggest change in his lifetime his immediate response was "These days we have to pay for labour. Years ago we just helped each other." And of course the regular use of money for wages, instead of shared work and barter, has undoubtedly had an enormous social impact.

Photograph someone at Trosnant with the box Brownie

Threshing at Trosnant, November 1952
Back row: Farm-worker from Cwm Gwdi, Ray Phillips, Penry Davies, Teddy Davies, Penry John Davies, Bill Cutter, Jack Prytherch
(Bill and Jack brought the threshing machine)
Middle row: Tommy Davies, Ron Harris, Ivor Davies, Peter Davies, Tommy Phillips
Front row: Roy Jones, Penry Davies Senior

In the days before machinery, shearing and harvest were highly labour intensive activities. People had to rely on family and neighbours to help. A rota would be agreed and all the available man and woman-power would descend on each farm in turn. Some people were allowed to plant a row of potatoes on one of the farms in return for helping the farmer bring in the hay and corn.

But threshing, shearing and harvest were not just jobs to be done; they were also great highlights of the social calendar. Huge amounts of food were cooked in each farm kitchen, with everyone joining in what became an annual round of wonderful communal meals.

Even the lack of refrigeration played a part in the sharing, bartering economy, with fresh food, like parts of the pig, being given away to save it going off, safe in the knowledge that the favour would be returned.

Photograph Teddy Davies, Trosnant.

Ready with a meal 1952
Back row: Phyllis Price, Eira Jones, Colin Jones,
Emily Davies, Hilda Williams, Joan James
Front row: Margaret Price, Michael Price, Emily Davies

What Ivor Phillips acutely observed was borne out in a study by Welsh historian Dr Elwyn Bowen who describes how, "The products of craftsmen such as tanners or weavers could be used by other local craftsmen. In many cases these craftsmen would not always be paid in cash but would receive corn or wool in return for their labour".

Life in a small community meant that the craftsmen would be all too aware of who was rich and who was poor; who could afford to pay and who could not. And according to Dr Bowen, "prices were adjusted to permit a reasonable living for the craftsman while taking into account the economic problems of his customer."

He cites the carpenters in Libanus as one example of this: when it came to pricing coffins, these carpenters "operated some form of sliding scale of charges for those in poor circumstances."

It's easy to look back at those days with rose-tinted spectacles. For all the community spirit and mutual co-operation, life in rural Breconshire was tough. An iron worker in the South Wales Valleys could earn three times as much as a farm labourer. Not suprising that the lure of the Valleys proved irresistible.

Dr Bowen: "Welsh rural communities lived almost perpetually under the threat of poverty and starvation. This background of insecurity and a life of ceaseless toil encouraged the movement of workers to the industrialised areas in search of better wages and prospects.

"In the period 1871–81, 3,600 adults left Breconshire for Glamorgan. This number increased to 4,300 between 1881-1891. Shortage of manpower resulted in higher wages for farm labourers, and this no doubt encouraged farmers to concentrate on livestock husbandry in Breconshire."

The migration of craftsmen to the new industrial areas, combined with the construction of canals, roads and railways to bring goods both in and out of the rural areas, was the beginning of the end of self-sufficient communities.

On the positive side, the burgeoning population attracted by the mines and ironworks needed food, and Breconshire was ideally placed to provide it. This was a big market opportunity.

Dr Elwyn Bowen's book is 'Traditional Industries of Rural Wales – Self-Sufficiency to Dependency in the County of Brecon'.

Transport – Opening Up the Beacons

To exploit the fast growing market in South Wales, what the farmers in the Beacons needed was good transport. In the 18th century the far-sighted Brecknock Agricultural Society had set as one of its goals the improvement of roads. But even so it was cheaper to get goods to the South Wales Valley from just about anywhere else than to get them from the nearest producers in Breconshire.

For instance, Dr Bowen, records that a ton of goods could be conveyed from Ireland for six to seven shillings per ton, whereas a haulier from Brecon would charge from twenty to twenty-five shillings per ton. In 1859, haulage of flour from Brecon was 2s 6d a sack, but from Bridgwater only 9d to 10d per sack and from Ireland 1s 3d per sack.

It was the building of a network of canals, tramways and railways that opened up the Beacons and transformed the local economy. First came the completion of the Monmouthshire and Brecon Canal in 1812. Barges carried coal and lime and also timber, iron, bricks, slates and manufactured goods.

Photograph Joyce Jenkins

The Monmouthshire and Brecon Canal celebrates its 200th anniversary in 2012

The Hay and Brecon Tram Road, from the Brecon canal wharves to Hay, opened in 1816. The Tram Road closed in the early 1860s when the Brecon & Merthyr Railway was built, in many places following the same route as the tram track.

Breakneck and Murder!

Building a railway to cross the Brecon Beacons was just the sort of challenge the Victorians loved. When it was finished, the Brecon & Merthyr Railway boasted the highest tunnel in the country, at 1,313 feet above sea level, and one of the steepest gradients on the UK's standard gauge network

From Talybont to Torpantau ('Seven Mile Bank') the average gradient was 1 in 47 and at its steepest 1 in 37. Often two and sometimes three engines were needed to pull the train. This was the second longest steep climb in Britain, with only Shap Fell in the Lake District being more severe.

Not surprisingly, given the gradient, there was a large number of runaway accidents, which earned the railway the disconcerting nickname, 'Breakneck and Murder'. The worst tragedy was on 2nd December 1878 when four people were killed.

The line through Talybont station was doubled and progressively lengthened across the river and up towards Pennorth, so that runaway engines could slow down on the uphill gradient without hitting anything in the meantime!

Photograph courtesy of Brecknock Museum

The steam locomotive Cymbeline was in regular service
On the Brecon and Merthy Railway 1866–1889

Meat Not Wheat

The new transport links transformed the economy of the Brecon Beacons. After the opening of the railway, residents in Breconshire could get coal at Talybont-on-Usk for 9s.8d (48p) a ton. Before the railway they had paid 23s.6d (£1.18p) a ton. Lime (used as fertilizer) reduced in price from 1s 3d(6p) a barrel to 10d (4p).*

Gathering sheep in the Taf Fechan Valley – above the Brecon & Merthyr Railway
The railway and canal brought in cheaper flour, enabling farmers to use the land to graze stock

But it was the ease and the cheapness of importing flour, which had the most dramatic impact on farming in the Brecon Beacons. Transporting large amounts of corn and wheat over the Beacons was difficult, so communities needed to grow their own crops in order to be self-sufficient. As early as the 12th century Geraldus recorded that "the region produces a great deal of corn."

In spite of the fact that more than half the land in Breconshire is above 1000 feet and a lot of it above 1500 feet, growing wheat and corn used to be a large part of the farming economy.

The Williams family at Priory Mill – around the time it closed in the 1930s
Behind: Bill Williams: In front: Tom, Nancy, Mother, Bill and young Beatrice

Priory Mill 2011

Mills were an essential part of the functioning of every community. Just as the drovers were responsible for farmers' stock so the millers were custodians of their crops. They too had to be people of great integrity and unimpeachable character.

Two of the most prominent were William Webb of Brecon and Hay (died 1880) and John Handley, the owner of Priory Mill, Brecon (died 1890). Webb left £7,000 and Handley £6825. Dr Elwyn Bowen[*] wrote "These were the highest recorded amounts for any craftsman, mercer or 'gent' of their day." To be a miller was to be one of the most prosperous and respected members of society.

But the opening up of the Beacons by canal and train was to be their death knell. Suddenly everything changed. Importing flour became a far cheaper and easier option than growing wheat and milling it locally. Farmers could concentrate on using their land for the kind of agriculture that suited it best – grazing sheep, cattle and horses.

In short it was more profitable to buy imported flour with the money made from livestock than to struggle to grow wheat on the difficult terrain of a hill farm. As arable acres declined so acres of pasture increased. So did the numbers of sheep and cattle in the Brecon Beacons.

It wasn't good news for the millers. In 1868 more than 11,000 acres of wheat were grown in Breconshire. By 1939 it was down to 595 and the importing of foreign flour had deprived the millers of a livelihood. Priory Mill in Brecon stopped milling wheat in the 1920s and feed for animals in the 1930s. Mills all over the county, including those at Abercynrig and Llanhamlach, met a similar fate.

Today most mills have either decayed or been converted into homes. But one of the oldest, Priory Mill, on the banks of the Honddu, is being carefully restored by Susie and Noel Gaskell. There has certainly been a mill here since 1651 but it seems probable that when Brecon Priory (now the Cathedral) was founded in 1100, this would have been the site of a much earlier Priory Mill.

Susie and Noel bought the Mill in 2000 from the Williams family, making them only the second owners in 100 years. When the mill ceased operating the Williams family continued running it as a smallholding with Mr Williams, well known for his milk round, known as Tom the Milk.

Today the Gaskells have carefully retained the old cobbled courtyard and are restoring the mill and surrounding buildings as authentically as possible. One day they hope to grind their flour again.

* Dr Elwyn Bowen 'Traditional Industries of Rural Wales'

By the late 1930s there were hardly any mills working in the Brecon Beacons. But just as they had their day, so then did the railway.

Most people think it was Dr Beeching who axed the Brecon & Merthyr Railway – but in fact it was closed in December 1962, four months before the publication of the first Beeching Report. The rails were ripped up and sold to farmers.

Though the railway track is long gone, the Talyllyn Tunnel, through which the line ran, is still there, on land that is part of Greenway Farm, Llanhamlach. Originally the tunnel was built in 1816 for horse-drawn trams, then when the railway arrived the track was altered the to take the trains. The tunnel is 674 yards (616 metres) long and became the oldest tunnel in regular use on Britain's railways. Today it is home to a colony of horseshoe bats.

Photograph Susan Brook

The entrance to Talyllyn Tunnel, Greenway Farm, Llanhamlach.

Greenway Farm

When Ben Williams' father Bryan bought Greenway Farm, through which the Talyllyn Tunnel runs, he bought more than a house with 325 acres and a piece of Welsh history; he also acquired a way to get served a drink on Sundays in the days when pubs in Wales were shut on the Sabbath.

The farm was one of many on the Peterstone Estate owned by Lord Glanusk, which were sold in the famous sale in July 1919 *(see page 17)*. The coal company Powell Duffryn bought Greenway that day – for £6,800 - a seemingly strange purchase for a company making its huge profits mining steam coal in the South Wales Valleys.

But Greenway was attractive to Powell Duffryn because it was on the newly opened Brecon & Merthyr Railway line – which meant quick transport to the farm for large numbers of pit ponies.

It is thought that the ponies came up regularly for breaks from working in the mines. But what is certain is that 500 of them were sent to the farm in 1926 for the duration of the General Strike. Ben says his grandfather believed that Powell Duffryn had foreseen the long strike and had bought Greenway in anticipation of needing a place to put the ponies for the duration.

The ponies grazed the land heavily and when they had eaten all the grass they started eating their way through the hedges – some of the gaps are still there. Fodder had to be brought in by the trainload to feed them and large numbers of tin sheds were erected to stable the ponies during the winter.

In 1932 Powell Duffryn decided it no longer needed the farm for the pit ponies, and Phillip Williams moved in as their tenant. He died in 1938 when Bryan was just 14 years old. It cut off Bryan's chances of any further education, so with the help of his mother and advice from his grandfather, he taught himself to run the farm. After World War II, when the coalmines were nationalised, Powell Duffryn sold Greenway to the Williams family.

Farming today is a very different job from the one Bryan Williams faced in the 1930s. Ben says that whilst he spends hours a week in his office, filling in forms and staying on the right side of all the current regulations, his father did it all by gut instinct. " He would have done some of it on the back of an envelope – but mostly in his head," says his son.

In the 1960s Bryan purchased Highgrove Farm next door and today Bryan's sons, Ben and Phillip, run both in tandem.

The Williams family
Ben, Kathryn, Phillip and Bryan Williams MFH

One of the great loves of the family has always been horses and hunting. And though they were not a family which took lots of photographs this one of Bryan Williams when he was Master of Fox Hounds with his three children, Ben, Kathryn and Philip has pride of place in their sitting room.

And as for that Sunday drink? *(Turn to page 184 .to find out how he did it.)*

With thanks to Kate Williams who wrote a project on her family and the farm when she was 10.

Welsh Mountain Ponies

With thanks to Colin Thomas, Welsh Mountain Pony Society
and Sarah Osbourne of the Cui Stud, Talybont-on-Usk

Photograph Dewi Thomas

Walking on the Brecon Beacons and rounding a corner or cresting a hill can bring you suddenly face to face with a group of these intelligent, gentle creatures; they make a heart-stopping sight. For more than a thousand years the Welsh Mountain Pony has fought heroically against the toughest conditions and the harshest of enemies, and won.

The breed had a big fan in Julius Caesar. When he and his armies saw the determined and courageous ponies drawing the chariots that opposed him he was so impressed he took many of them back to Rome.

59

Small and sturdy, the breed is ideally suited to the meagre pickings to be found on the Beacons – these ponies can thrive on poor quality forage, which makes them perfect for grazing the hills, encouraging wildflowers, heather and wild grasses. Tough winter coats mean they can live outside in the coldest of winters – though they prefer frost and snow to rain. The characteristics of the breed as it is known today were probably established by the late 15th century, after the Crusaders returned to Britain with Arab stallions obtained from the Middle East.

But in the 16th century they faced a real threat of extinction. King Henry VIII, thinking to improve the breeds of horses, particularly war-horses, ordered the destruction of all stallions under 15 hands and all mares under 13 hands. This could have been curtains for the small Welsh Mountain Pony. Thankfully the wild, remote, and inaccessible mountains of Wales provided the perfect escape and refuge.

The Welsh Mountain Pony was an essential part of hill farming life for centuries. They were used for a huge variety of work; from shepherding to ploughing to carrying a farmer to market or driving a family in a trap to services on Sunday.

Photograph courtesy of the Clark family

Horse Fair in Llanfaes, Brecon

In towns they drew the carts of hawkers, butchers and rag-and-bone men. They also made great pets. Their popularity grew to such a degree that at horse fairs such as the one in Llanfaes, Brecon, the streets were packed with traders and onlookers.

Driving past the Storey Arms on the A470, look towards the Beacons and you may see a herd of Welsh Mountain Ponies, which has belonged to the Powell family since the 1930s. In 1952 Baden (Bud) Powell and his wife Mary moved to Penstar and Bud became one of the most respected breeders of mountain ponies in the Beacons.

Baden (Bud) Powell, Penstar, at Vaynor Show in the 1950s
Hetty Mackay-Smith, from Farnley, Virginia, USA, is judging

61

Welsh Mountain Pony boarding a train at Talybont-on-Usk,
bound for Liverpool Docks and then the USA

Many of the ponies went abroad, to America in particular. Bud said that exporting ponies was the highlight of his breeding career. He was proud of selling four ponies to Denmark for £1000 in 1969, which enabled him to buy the sheep to stock Cwm Llwch (The Loggin), which the family had just acquired. Bud died in 2010. His son Colin with his wife Sheila and their son Gareth have taken up the reins.

In the Beacons, the name Richards is synonymous with Welsh Mountain Ponies. The Richards family founded the world famous Criban Stud at Abercriban Farm in the Taf Fechan Valley When the valley was flooded, they moved to Talybont-on-Usk and continued the tradition, founding the Cui Stud, which today is run by Howell Richards' granddaughter Sarah. For Sarah and her sisters Libby and Jill, Welsh Mountain Ponies were an integral part of life on a hill farm.

Sarah, Jill and Libby Richards, gathering ponies from the hill. 1950s

The future of the Welsh Mountain Pony is largely in the capable hands of the Welsh Mountain Pony and Cob Society and a number of Hill Pony Improvement Societies in the Brecon Beacons. They ensure good breeding practices and good animal welfare.

Today the ponies all need passports and have to be registered and chipped, at a cost of £35 each, which is considered a heavy premium and drives prices down. At a Derogation sale in Brecon in 2010 some ponies were sold for as little as £3. It's a tough time for the Welsh Mountain Pony – but he's a survivor, always has been.

Richard (Dick) Tyle Llwyd

Richard Davies, Tyle Llwyd, Cantref (Dick Tyle Llwyd,) was another who was famous as a breeder of Welsh Mountain Ponies, and in 1920 he registered his first ponies with the Welsh Pony and Cob Society, under the prefix 'Tyle'.

An article in The Welsh Pony and Cob Society Journal reported, "The sheep and pony walk at Tyle Llwyd runs up to the Cribyn, one of the three peaks of the Beacons and the steepest and roughest part of these hills. Here a quick, sure-footed pony is essential for shepherding, especially at the time of year when sheep and ponies are gathered."

Richard Davies (Dick Tyle Llwyd)
1889 – 1969

It's an overused word, but to say Dick Tyle Llwyd was 'a character', seems absolutely right. Everyone who knew him has fond memories of Eliza Davies' (see pages 20 and 21) youngest son. Eirwen Stephens, Bailea, describes her neighbour as, "A true Welshman, Welsh-speaking, not very tall, with a round happy face and kind personality."

When Dick was seventeen he went to the South Wales Valleys to find work, and became a wrestling champion. The winner of wrestling matches in those days was the last man left standing. Dick became the champion of the GWR repair shed at Neath, having eliminated two hundred opponents to acquire the title.

Dick joined his mother at Tyle Llwyd shortly before she died in 1922. Afterwards he farmed alone until his bachelor brother David (Dai) joined him in 1940. They farmed together there for the next thirty years, with their sister Bessie and her husband Tom Phillips as close neighbours at Bailea. Tom was the brother of Price Phillips (see pages 23 and 77).

Dick's nephew, Jonathan Davies of Brychgoed Farm, Senni, had very fond memories of the man he described as "My favourite uncle. As a cavalryman (see pages 22 and 23), he was a keen horseman and I remember two horses in particular: Bount the cart mare and Chess the Welsh cob. They would convey him weekly on Fridays in the trap to Brecon to get the groceries, which would break the monotony of life on a remote hill farm high in the Brecon Beacons.

"He lived a hard bachelor life with his brother, and was always popular with his neighbours, to whom he was greatly indebted. He was a jovial person and always happy with his ponies and his lurcher dogs, so renowned for keeping down the fox population. Being of a humorous nature he was very good at saying wits at concerts and local eisteddfodau."

Austin Morgan, Tynllwyn, remembered the warm welcome at Dick's farmhouse, where fresh bracken was piled on the floor for the dogs to sleep on. The fire was kept burning by pushing a whole tree up the chimney and letting it burn down slowly.

Everywhere Dick went, his dogs accompanied him. One of the most astonishing stories was reported in 1965 in the Welsh Pony and Cob Journal - "At the beginning of the last world war there was no further hunting on the Beacons and foxes increased rapidly. Mr. Davies then bought a lurcher (greyhound-sheepdog cross), which he named 'Blucher'. This remarkable dog, aided by the sheepdog, killed 140 full-grown foxes."

In those days lambing was done out of doors, on the hill, and the threat posed by foxes was great. Fox Clubs were formed by groups of farmers who each paid some money into a kitty. Anyone who killed a fox would be rewarded with £1 upon presentation of the fox's tail. Dick was so successful at ridding the hills of foxes that his neighbours made him a presentation in appreciation.

The Testimonial to Richard (Dick) Davies
From his Neighbours and Friends

The last word goes to Dick's nephew, Jonathan: "He may have lacked education in his young days but he was blessed with a colourful character. Not the least, he was a member of The Plough and Twyn Congregational Chapels. Perhaps modern education tends to streamline people like peas in a pod. He was laid to rest in the family burial ground at Brychgoed Chapel in 1969."

Ploughing a Lonely Furrow

Up and down, up and down, up and down, hour after hour after hour, concentrating every step of the way on the contour of the land and the line of the furrow. Ploughing and drilling look like the loneliest jobs in farming.

Ronny Stephens drilling swedes at Cwmcynwyn 1962

It is astonishing that the design of the tool used to do the job, the plough, changed so little for more than fifteen hundred years. In fact you have to go back to 50 BC to find the origin of the plough that was used in Wales until the eighteenth century.

Even in the early 1900s farmers were using ploughs almost identical to the large heavy ploughs developed on the continent and brought here in about 50 BC by the Belgue.

These huge ploughs needed up to eight oxen to pull them, with three or four men to control the oxen. Walter Davies (Walter Mechanic) said of the Welsh plough "A more awkward tool is not to be found in any civilised country. It is not calculated to cut a furrow; but to tear it open by main force. A field ploughed with this machine looks as if a drove of swine had been moiling it."

In 1755 a group of progressive, public-spirited landowners decided it was time to import the latest agricultural methods in farming into the county. They founded the Brecknockshire Agricultural Society, now the oldest agricultural society in England and Wales, and began the education of farmers and tenants in modern ways of growing crops and rearing livestock.

The Society met at the Golden Lion in Lion Street and by the end of the 18th century many farmers had improved their expertise and the Society decided to set up a library in the pub. They spent 30 guineas on agricultural books followed by more money on volumes on manures and drainage.

Photograph courtesy of 'Amgueddfa Ceredigion Museum, Aberystwyth'

Oxen ploughing with the old "Welsh Plough" 1910

And in 1774 the Society brought in a new kind of plough, the swing plough, which could be pulled by horses. One can only imagine the joy of farmers when it arrived, and although the first ploughs were tricky to handle, they were soon improved by adding wheels that made them much easier to control.

These light ploughs proved popular and the Society gave a prize of £4 to the farmer who ploughed the greatest acreage, above 10 acres, with a plough drawn by two horses or two oxen working abreast[*].

In 1839, at the Brecon Agricultural Society's Annual Show, the best ploughman received a suit of clothes, the second prize was a coat and waistcoat and the third prize was a coat. The buttons on these coats had a plough embossed on each, with the name of the Society surrounding the plough[*].

William Gwyn Davies, Gelli Farm, Hirwaun, ploughing with Jolly and Brown in the British National Ploughing Championships 1969

Today ploughing with the swing plough and horses is a hotly contested activity with national and international competitions attracting farmers and spectators from around the world.

Since the introduction of tractors, after the Second World War, ploughing has been revolutionised with ploughs that can cut three or four furrows at a time.

[*] *Leslie Williams' book 'The Guiding Light, Brecknockshire Agricultural Society 1755-2005'*

Today the state-of-the-art, top-of-the-range tractor plough can even plough in reverse and makes straight furrows of a field in no time!

And the job is made less lonely these days because in the cosy air-conditioned, heated and weatherproof cabin, there is of course a radio!

Horses

Imagine a countryside where the sounds and smells were of horses instead of engines, and the lanes only had to be wide enough for a pony and trap. Every decent sized farm probably boasted at least two teams of working shire horses (two in each team) to work the land.

Horses and Welsh Mountain Ponies were used for riding, hunting, pulling coaches, carts, gambos and traps.

Austin Morgan was born in Tynllwyn in 1926. Travelling by pony and trap provided him with one of his earliest memories: " I have a vivid picture in my mind of travelling from Tynllwyn to the Methodist Chapel in Pencelli on Sunday morning.

"Our trap was not very posh compared with the tub traps that many people had, with a plush seat right around the tub. Ours had a wide wooden plank across the middle. My mother and father sat facing forward and we three children sat facing backwards, unless it was raining. Then we three kids would squat underneath the wooden plank. Looking back now, I am very impressed with the effort my parents made to get to Chapel each Sunday, without fail. To travel by pony and trap over the distance of three and a half miles each way would take a while."

A Royal Commission counted the number of horses in Breconshire between 1911-13 at 13,090. That was horsepower at its peak. When the first tractor came to Tregaer there were four horses working on the farm. The tractor replaced three of them. It was a story repeated everywhere. By 1939 the number of horses in the county had reduced to 9,875.

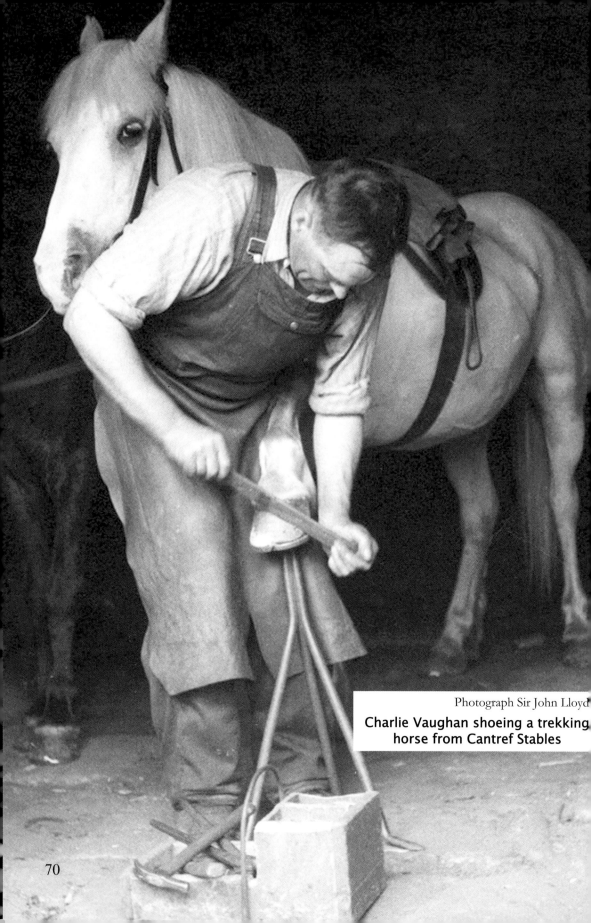

Charlie Vaughan shoeing a trekking horse from Cantref Stables

The Blacksmith

The Welsh have always given craftsmen such as wheelwrights, millers, tanners and blacksmiths an honourable status in society. In fact the blacksmith, along with the bard, were the two most important officials at court under the old Welsh laws of Hwyel Dda.

Forges were great talking shops, the water coolers of their day. This was where news and gossip were exchanged, accompanied by the ringing blows of the hammer. Today the Three Horseshoes in Groesffordd and the White Swan in Llanfrynach remain places for locals and visitors to gather – though the smithies are long gone.

The Three Horseshoes started life as a house called Tŷr y Groesffordd (house on the crossways). It was right next to Groesffordd Halt railway station and many locals still call the pub The Groesffordd. In 1846 a local blacksmith, David Powell, opened a smithy and an inn at the house and called it the Three Horseshoes. The name comes from the obvious fact that when a horse arrives in need of a shoe, it comes with Three Horseshoes.

The White Swan was the home of more than one generation of blacksmiths of the Davies family, and it seems likely that the pub was a sideline to the smithy, probably run by the women of the household. As it was the smith to whom people turned when they needed a tooth pulled, the neighbouring pub would surely have been a blessing!

Bill Vaughan's father Charlie founded the forge in Cantref in the middle of the 1800s. The forge, like most other things in the area, was silent on Sundays, when instead of ringing hammer-blows on his anvil, Bill rang the bells at Cantref Church, which he did for 50 years. He and his wife Margaret had four children: Charlie, who took over as blacksmith, Muriel, Idris and Hannah.

Charlie Vaughan had a big influence on the life of David Thomas, now Revd Thomas, who grew up at Tir-y-Groes, Cantref. David wrote: "Generations of children spent hours watching Charlie working, shoeing horses and making all sorts of things. My mother and I were just two of those who loved to listen to Charlie's stories, for he was always so full of fun. He was much loved by us, and it was his example and encouragement, which played an important part in my eventually seeking ordination.

"One of the greatest losses to the community in my lifetime was the closure of the forge in Cantref. For generations it had proved a focal point for the community. With his death, just before his sixty-fifth birthday in 1979, came the end of an era."

**Charlie Vaughan and his father Bill at the Forge
Putting new Shafts in the Gambo**

Charlie was one of the last of his kind. The census returns for 1841 and 1881 show that the number of blacksmiths in Breconshire fell from 374 to 257, and it was to plummet still further.

The loss of the blacksmith and other traditional craftsmen happened quickly. They had depended on each other. The blacksmith banded the wheelwright's wheel; the farrier shod the oxen, which later provided the tanner with skins who in turn supplied the shoemaker and saddler with leather. The limestone-burner and charcoal burner provided essential materials for the ironworker who produced iron for the blacksmith to make implements. When any one left the domino effect was inevitable.

Historian Dr Elwyn Bowen wrote, "These craftsmen provided a necessary infrastructure for the efficient functioning of a rural society."

The Combustion Engine Arrives

The arrival of the combustion engine was to mean a big change for ordinary country folk. But before cars and tractors became commonplace in farms and villages those who could afford the very best were having a love affair with a fabulous array of motor transport. Major John Lloyd (later to become Sir John), Abercynrig was a real enthusiast.

He was also an enthusiastic photographer and probably took this photograph under which he wrote that they were on their way to a meeting (presumably a race meeting) at Ludlow when they had a puncture in Glasbury. He obviously got out to record the scene while the chauffeur did the necessary repair.

Photograph Major John Lloyd

Running Repair
The registration number is EU 147   The photograph was taken in 1907

**Hollow (the chauffeur), Rev Saunders–Jones (Rector of Cantref),
Brace, Major John Lloyd**

No-one knows where this was taken or by whom. But it shows Major John Lloyd with Revd Saunders- Jones, the Rector of Cantref, wearing the most amazing driving coat along with another gentleman called Brace – and behind the car Hollow, the chauffeur.

Until 1923 Cantref had its own Rector and Cantref used to be considered a much richer living than Llanfrynach. That all came to an end in 1923 when the Church in Wales became disestablished and disendowed. Revd Saunders-Jones was the last Rector to have the sole living of Cantref. A plaque in the Church commemorates his son St John who was killed in action in East Africa in 1917.

Photograph Major John Lloyd

A golden moment in the sun in a wonderful motorcar.
Marie and Conway Lloyd in a Lagonda at Dinas in 1937

The next cars to arrive in Llanfrynach and Cantref were probably in 1928. They belonged to Bill Price of Upper Cantref, who bought a Morris Oxford, EU4991, and Thomas Morgan, Tynllwyn, a Morris Cowley, TX4262. William Powell, Pentwyn, bought the third car.

Bill Price's daughter Jean Phillips remembers her father going on a train to Hereford market in 1928: "In a mad moment he decided to buy a car. He drove home with the salesman from the garage, his one and only lesson, arriving back at Brecon station where the salesman caught the train back to Hereford."

The arrival of the first car at Tynllwyn made a big impression on a young Austin Morgan: "My father said he was not pleased because he did not know what the clutch did or what was underneath the gear lever. He said he soon found out that the car never listened to him when he said 'Whoa, whoa!'

Much against his pride, he had to ask the work boy who rode a motorbike to teach him the basics of the engine and the pedals, teach him what made the car move forward, and at what speed. The car was driven a grand total of seventeen miles per week. Seven miles to and from Chapel every Sunday and 10 miles return trip to Brecon every Friday, which was market day."

Price Phillips, Caerau, with
Joy and Jewel 1953

Changing Gear

Change can be difficult. Not everyone embraces it enthusiastically and the change of gear from horses to cars and tractors proved a real challenge to many.

After the First World War Price Phillips *(see page 22)* returned to work at Pannau Farm before taking on the tenancy of Caerau, Llanfrynach. He loved his two horses, Joy and Jewel, and never really came to terms with the need to drive. His daughter Barbara Jones said that when the day came for him to retire and the contents of the farm were sold, the greatest wrench was to sell the horses. Joy went for £24 and Jewel for £18. "He was heartbroken", she said.

The first two tractors arrived in the area in 1938, an Allis-Chalmers and a Ford owned by Bill Price and Mr Morgan, Pannau, respectively. By the end of the Second World War the use of the combustion engine on the farm was well and truly established, the days of the workhorse over, and one of the chief desires of most farmers was to own a shiny brand new Ferguson tractor.

Emlyn Williams *(see his story p 106)* was working at Tregaer, Llanfrynach, when the farm's first tractor was purchased. Emlyn loved the four horses, two greys, one chestnut and one black, which were used for ploughing, harrowing and cutting corn. But the arrival of the tractor meant he had to say farewell to three of them.

As far as Emlyn was concerned, that was not good news at all. He has never learnt to drive a car. "Not interested," he said.

He did however learn to drive a scooter and then a motorbike. It took him three tries to pass his test. On the second attempt, Gwynne Griffiths, Tregaer, advised him, "Put your foot down – you can do it". But he returned home having failed again, explaining, "I was too much of a speed merchant" – and anyone who knows the quietly mannered Emlyn knows that's a description worth a laugh.

What Emlyn loved was to plough, harrow, cut corn and hay with horse power. He preferred the old fashioned, traditional ways of farming – everything from cropping and laying hedges to shearing sheep – jobs many of which, he says, were better done by hand.

But not everyone was so reluctant to embrace the combustion engine revolution. Gwen and Dilwyn Williams had settled down to married life at Bryn Balgoed, Libanus, when in 1945 the first tractor arrived on the farm. Gwen said, "It was wonderful. Dilwyn had never driven before. A man came from Brecon to show him."

And everyone drove the tractor: their four sons, Glyn, Keith, Bryan and Gordon, and Gwen herself. Only men tackled the heavy and skilled job of ploughing. But the women used the tractor for harrowing, rolling and loading hay.

**Mary Phillips (now Mary Owen–Lowe)
With her Singer – 1941**

Glyn Owen–Lowe

One of the first women to own a motorcar must have been Mary Phillips of Pontbrengarreg. In 1941 she had a Singer, which she says she absolutely loved. Before the Second World War, she married a man who was to spend his working life selling motorcycles, tractors and farm machinery.

Glyn Owen-Lowe still has his Defence of the Realm Driving Licence, which he bought for five shillings just before war broke out. He just missed being first in the queue. His number was 002.

In 2011 Glyn, now 91, and Mary, 89, are still motoring on. They celebrate their 68th wedding anniversary this year.

And cars are still at the heart of family life: their daughter Sheila is married to Peter Jenkins, and together they run Brecon Car Sales. Their daughter Lara and son Robert work with them and Rob has picked up the driving baton, becoming a rally driver.

**Glyn and Mary Owen Lowe
on their Diamond Wedding Day**

No Mod Cons

Go to any WI meeting in the Brecon Beacons and you will meet women who brought up children and ran homes with no running water or electricity.

Barbara Jones was born in 1929 in the minute house attached to the Chapel in Cantref – Capel Twyn. Her parents Price Phillips *(see pages 22 and 77)* and his wife Winifred were absolutely thrilled when they became tenants of Caerau Farm, Llanfrynach, when she and her sister Gaynor were quite young. But though their new home might have been an improvement on the old, it was still very old fashioned.

In common with most other farms, all water had to be carried to the house – drinking water from a well and other water from the river. Winifred milked the cows, made butter, lit the bread oven once a week to bake the week's supply, and washed clothes by hand. And like many other farmer's wives she never shied away from the work that had to be done in the fields.

The only heat came from a fire around which the family gathered – and when a guest arrived the family moved round so that the visitor could be given the warmest place to sit. Barbara remembers the flames of a fire flickering in her parent's bedroom when her youngest sister was born in a snowy November. The new baby was called Eira (Welsh for snow) and was always known as Eira Caerau.

Of course, there was no television, but eventually a battery-operated radio arrived and Barbara recalls having to go to Brecon for batteries and how very heavy they were.

When June Smith married Teddy Davies and went to live at Trosnant Farm, Cantref, in 1958, it must have been like turning the clock back a hundred years. As a maid at Tŷ Fry Farm, she had been used to the mod-cons of the twentieth century. At Trosnant she was faced with a home with no bathroom, no electricity and no hot water.

She is astonished, looking back, at how much the life and the produce of the farm actually came into the house. "After threshing, the oats were carried through the front room and up the stairs to be stored in what was the granary. After shearing, all the fleeces would be brought through the house and stored in the big attic. This was in the days when the price of wool was so low it couldn't be sold. The feathering of geese happened in the back kitchen."

Electricity came to Llanfrynach in 1938, and to Cantref in 1959/60, though Bailea and Cwmcynwyn did not get it until 1966.

Servants

The lack of labour saving devices, even of running water, meant that employing people to deal with the daily mountain of chores was essential.

In 1891, four servants were living in the house at Tŷ Fry Farm. But it wasn't just the big farms that had this kind of help. Even the smallest usually had at least one live-in maid. And at the other end of the scale the big houses in the village employed lots of help.

The de Winton family moved to their town house in Brecon for the winter months and let their country residence. This is shown in the 1891 census, when William Baxter, who had two daughters living with him, occupied Maesderwen and maintained a staff of nine, made up of a lady's maid, a cook, two housemaids, a kitchen maid and a footman. A groom, coachman and gardener were resident in cottages adjacent to the house.

At Tŷ Mawr, Miss Dona and Miss Alice de Winton kept the estate immaculate with the help of a kitchen maid, a cook, housemaid, parlour maid, chauffeur, gardener and under-gardener.

This is a description by Mary Davies of life as an 18-year-old girl in service at Abercriban Farm, as told to Libby Richards: "I slept in one of the attic bedrooms and we were not allowed to use the new bathroom; we had to get water in a jug for washing in our room. I earned £3 a month, worked every day from 6am until 9pm, with one afternoon off a week. I was not allowed to whistle or sing. I stayed for seven years and left to get married."

Elma Higgins knew nothing about the country when she arrived at Greenway in Llanhamlach aged fourteen years old to be a maid. Elma was born in Aberfan in the Vale of Merthyr. Her father was a coal-miner and a preacher in the local Chapel. When she left school Elma worked for a while in a factory, but it didn't suit her, and she became ill. Eventually a friend who had gone to work as a maid in another farm told her of the vacancy and Elma decided to try it.

She soon got used to the housework. She learnt to deal with the chickens, also with the turkeys, which came into fashion while she was working there. But she is still petrified of geese!

John Jones (1872-1934) a gardener at Abercynrig
On the Bridge in Llanfrynach

Elbow Grease

From childhood to old age everyone who could work in the countryside would have to do their bit. Being involved with the work of the farm would be part and parcel of growing up. Even after a life of hard physical work retirement was a luxury. Although paupers could receive some Parish Relief, this would have been barely sufficient to exist on, and some men are mentioned in the census returns as still being agricultural labourers at the age of seventy-five years or more.

When Gwen Williams, Capel Twyn, Cantref, was five years old, her grandfather, William Williams, The Wern, Cantref, died and Gwen's family moved to the Wern. Her widowed grandmother Rachel moved to the Rhiwiau where she lived alone, though one of her grandchildren (Gwen or her brothers Lewis and Leslie) always slept overnight with her.

Gwen, who celebrates her 90th birthday in 2011, says life then was very quiet. Like other farms they did something of everything: sheep, cattle, ducks, geese, chickens, pigs – they all required looking after and she and her brothers "jolly well had to help".

**Gwennie Williams and her grandmother Rachel
outside the Rhiwiau, Llanfrynach, c 1920**

When butter was to be made, Gwen was sent to collect cold water from an old well near to Tyle Llwyd. It was probably fed by a spring and had a spout, the water from which made a small stream. Water cold enough to make butter came from there or from the Roman well at the Rhiwiau. Gwen milked the cows and liked it; but she hated milking the ewes – "dirty, smelly things". Cheese and butter were made from the milk of both cows and ewes.

The work that girls like Gwen did at home prepared them for work as maids on other farms and in big houses. Gwen said, "It was hard work. People today say they are busy; but it's not the same – this was hard work. You just had to keep on going until you finished the job."

Something Gwen and Glenys Pugh (née Evans) both remember vividly is the incredible watercress, which grew in a stream that ran by the road at Tyle Llwyd. They say its marvelous fresh peppery smell is something that has vanished from the watercress they buy today.

What of teenage years in the country? Gwen says all her friends had bikes, and on Saturday nights would go to one of the two cinemas in Brecon, the Coliseum, still going today, or the Palace, which was on the site now occupied by Aldi.

In common with most other girls in her circumstances, Gwen Williams not only left school when she was 14, but left home as well - to be a 'maiden' or maid. Gwen found a place at Tŷ Mawr Farm, where she did much the same kind of work as she had done at home, for which she was now paid £10 every six months. She already knew the family who farmed Tŷ Mawr and she settled in quickly.

But after six months Gwen's mother became ill and she returned home to look after the family. When her mother got better she went to work for the Prosser family at Lower Cwm Clyn, Libanus. It took her a bit longer to settle at this new farm, but it was here she met her husband-to-be, Dilwyn Williams, who lived on a neighbouring farm, Bryn Bolgoed.

Gwen had always worshipped at Cantref Church. It was where she had been christened and where she wanted to be married. But because her family home, The Wern, was then in the parish of Llanfrynach, she had to spend at least one night a week for three weeks sleeping in Cantref Parish. She duly spent her three nights as a guest at Pontbren Farm with her friend Mary Phillips (see page 78). So the Revd Perrot was able to conduct the wedding ceremony of Gwen Williams and Dilwyn Williams at Cantref Church, which meant that Gwen has always remained a Williams.

The wedding of Gwen Williams and Dilwyn Williams
Cantref Church, 22nd October 1941
Mary Owen Lowe (née Phillips) was bridesmaid

Childbirth

One of the major changes for women has been in the whole area of childbirth. In the days before contraception and a free National Health Service, large families were common, and so was the early death of a worn-out mother.

Sue Chamberlain of Cantref says her great-grandmother, who lived at Old Cwmcynwyn in 1886, died aged 37 after bearing 10 children. In Cefn Cantref, Ann Watkins died in her fifties after having 17 children. Her husband lived till he was 94. In Llanfrynach Elizabeth Grismond married John Phillips in 1681 and went on to have twenty children at single births and miscarried eleven times. The last child was a daughter, Phillippa, born in 1713.[*]

Abortion was illegal but not uncommon as a last resort, with women worn out by repeated childbirth and with no respite from the physical challenge of running a house and farm. One local woman was prosecuted for performing a termination and sent to prison.

But for the majority, being pregnant meant almost no change in the daily routine. Glenys Pugh and Gwen Williams said they just reported their condition to the doctor and got on with it. "You just kept working till it came."

Many women were happy to take advantage of a two-week stay in Brecon Hospital with a new baby as a welcome rest from housework and farming.

But with transport limited to either a pony and trap or sometimes a car, most babies were born at home. A doctor was an expensive luxury for anything but the most vital medical emergency. Two midwives in particular helped women in Llanfrynach and Cantref: Dinah Phillips, mother of Ivor Phillips of Tylebrythos, a farmers' wife, was first to be called when a baby was on the way. She was famous for running across the fields of Cantref to attend yet another birth.

The other, a professional midwife, was Nurse Peters, who lived in Llanfaes. Mary Owen-Lowe has the photograph of her with triplets, but no one seems to know who they were or what happened to them. Her charges are recorded, however, in an invoice dated 26th January 1931. Her bill was £4.10s. This was at the height of the depression when a wage of £3 a week was considered good, and £4 or £5 a week was riches indeed.

The baby who was the cause of this bill was Margaret Davies, now Margaret Price of Groesffordd, and a founder member of the Llanfrynach and Cantref WI.

[*] *Llanfrynach Church History Sep 2005 Edition – RJM Sinnett*

Nurse Peters
Brecon

No.   Date 26   1   193/

To Mr. Perry Davies

Trosnant Farm

Cantref Nr Brecon

...............weeks professional services

at...............per week   Confinement

Travelling Expenses   7/12/30

Laundry   visits

Extras   and car

	£	s.	d.
	4	10	0

Paid by A M Peters

....

Received with thanks   TOTAL

£ 4. 10 0

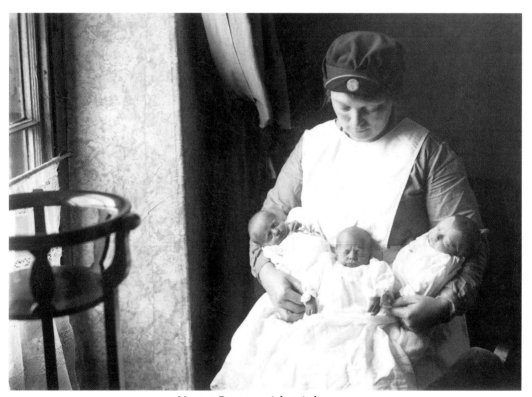

Nurse Peters with triplets

What We Are Called

Susan Brook

In town, people go by the name of their trade, Dai the Milk (Llanfaes Dairy), Dai Bandit (mended slot machines), Michael Mechanic (cars and farm machines), Evans Above (vicar) and Evans Below (undertaker) etc.

In the country, people get the name of their farm attached to them. In Cantref there are two women called Michelle Davies, each referred to by the name of their farm: Michelle Berllan and Michelle Pencaefadog. With so few names to go round (most residents are a Davies, a Williams, a Phillips or an Evans) it makes life easier to call people by their address.

For many years Bessie Phillips (sister to Dick Tyle Llwyd) lived at Bailea with her husband Tom (Price Phillips' brother). This photo says it all.

Bessie Bailea
Bessie Phillips (née Davies) – 1887 – 1971

When I had been living at Crofftau for a few years I was at a meeting of the Women's Institute and heard someone say, "Ask Sue Crofftau" and was thrilled to realise they were talking about me. It was like being accepted and included into some great local tribe.

At Cantref Sports 2010, one of the competitions for the children was to draw a map of Cantref – a task that would defeat many adults! One entry summed up the difference between a rural and an urban childhood. Robert Evans of New Croftau Farm drew all the lanes on his map. But instead of writing the name of each farm or house, he wrote the name of the people, mostly his friends, who lived there. Like all children here, he knows just who lives at each home and something about each of them.

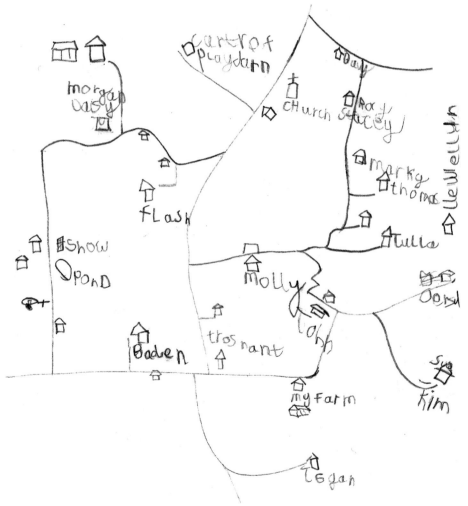

Robert Evans' map of Cantref
Featuring: Rory and Stacey, Marky, Thomas, Davy, Llywelyn, Morgan and Daisy, Flash, Molly, John, Baden, Tegan, Sue and Kim, Denzil, Cantref Playbarn, Trosant, the site of Libanus Show (Geoff Probert's smallholding), Church and My Farm (New Crofftau).

Keeping Up Appearances

A family gathering – the de Wintons on the lawn at Tŷ Mawr

Life in the country can often be dominated (on the sartorial front) by wellies and waterproofs. But the desire to 'keep up appearances' is strong. The Williams family dominated tailoring in Llanfrynach between 1841 and 1881. But there was also a seamstress from London, Ann Price, who visited Maesderwen, the home of the de Wintons. She was probably more skilled and fashionable than the local dressmakers and the clothes produced for the de Winton ladies were much grander than those made in the village for the farmers' wives and village women.

Rachel Williams at the Rhiwiau

Many old photographs show that even women with only a few pennies to spend on themselves and hard physical work to do were immaculately turned out.

Look at Gwen William's grandmother Rachel's beautifully laundered and ironed apron. Women did the hardest work in crisp, white caps, collars and aprons. Barbara Jones says ironing them with a flat iron, heated by the fire, was difficult and exhausting.

Maybe the daily need to put practicality and warmth before fashion is a particular reason the country community makes the most of any occasion to dress up.

Market day was a highlight of the week and warranted a good frock or suit. Margaret Jane Jones, grandmother of Denzil Stephens, Bailea, dressed smartly for the trip. But before setting off she put an old mac on for the journey of four or five miles from Fforest Farm, Crickadarn, to Erwood Market, carrying everything she had to sell on her pony.

Imagine travelling that distance with a heavy basket laden with butter, cheese and eggs on each arm, reins in each hand and a pony stick as well. On the right side of the pony (as you look) is a bag called a 'frail'. A pair of chicken legs is poking out of the top. Underneath the mac can just been seen a necklace and something smart. And in the stirrups her shoes are freshly polished.

Margaret Jane Jones Goes To Market

When Eliza Davies went to market she often had so little to sell that her grandson Selwyn Thomas said she would hide it in her gown to avoid having to pay the fee charged for selling produce in the market. And who can blame her when every penny she could earn meant so much.

But the desire to wear the right clothes at the right moment and to be properly turned out is deeply ingrained. In the days when mourning clothes were worn as a mark of grief and respect, Eliza had her photograph taken in what were known as 'widows weeds' – her very grand black gown is an astonishing contrast to her working clothes (see pages 20/21).

Photograph taken at Clarks' Photographic Studio

Eliza Davies, Tyle Llwyd, Llanfrynach. 1914

But it's not only the women who had style. There were, and are, plenty of dashing men about. Look at these wedding photographs.

On the right are Davis Lewis Morgan and Alice Price, Tregaer.

Her 1920s hat and frock were absolutely top fashion at the time. Her shoes with their fine buckles are lovely.

And Davis looks rather film-star-like in his sharp suit with a great hat in his hand.

They lived at Pannau until 1958, when their youngest daughter Eleanor and her husband Beynon took over. Their grandson David, his partner Jane and children Cathy, Morgan and Davey continue to farm there today.

Mr. and Mrs. Davis Morgan 1922

The wedding of Dai and Pats Phillips, The Neuadd, 1928
Gertrude, Dai, Pats, Bill, Mr Williams, Cwmcynwyn

Neuadd in Cantref probably dates back to the sixteenth century so it is not surprising that it is this house that has the 'King Charles II hid here' legend attached to it. None of that mattered on the day that Dai and Pats Phillips married – a handsome family group.

91

The Womens' Institute Remembers

By Susan Brook

The early success of many rural WIs must have been in part due to the fact that whilst men went to the livestock market and the pub, there were few occasions for women, who often led very isolated lives, to gather together socially. Maybe that is one reason why Cantref and Llanfrynach WI inspires such loyalty and friendship. In 2009 we celebrated 60th anniversary of the first meeting of our WI, held in Llanfrynach and Cantref Village Hall on 29th June 1949. Four of our founder members: Jean Phillips, Mary Owen-Lowe, Margaret Price and Joyce Williams were there.

Llanfrynach and Cantref Women's Institute's 60th Anniversary

Back row: Sheila Jenkins, Phylis Williams, June Davies, June Mathews, Pam Herring, Glenys Pugh, Sally Davies.
3rd row; Anthea Philliips, Jill Ward, Deirdre Hemmings, Barbara Smith, Sue Chamberlain, Mary Evans
2nd row: Val Jones, Elma Higgins, Eirwen Stephens, Val Williams, Joyce Griffiths, Myfanwy Davies, Olwyn Williams, Sheila Jarman, Jean Jones.
Front row: Diana Adams, Mary Owen-Lowe, Jean Phillips, Rose Morris (County chairman), Susan Brook, Joyce Williams, Margaret Price.

I thought it would be a good idea to record some of the old skills from the people who knew all about them first hand. So I asked the WI members to tell me how they made butter and what they did with the house pig. Well of course they all talked at once. And this is what I have made of it.

Making Butter

First milk the cow! Then take the milk to the separator, which divides the cream from the milk. If there isn't a separator then you let it cool and then scoop off the cream by hand.

Pat Eckley's Cream Separator

Let the cream stand for about a week. Then put it in a butter churn. The churn is a wooden barrel with a handle and a small glass spy hole in the top so you can see how the butter is doing.

To make the butter sounds hard work, but simple. Except that there's a knack!
> "Turn the handle until the cream has turned to butter!"
> "Fast to start and then slow!"
> "It takes longer to make the butter in hot weather – the colder the day the easier and quicker it is."
> "I used to get fed up of it."
> "Listen to it – hear if it's moving and it hasn't gone to sleep."
> "Jerk it back and forward!"

Well each person seemed to have her own way of doing it. But after the butter is churned what you have left is the buttermilk, which is terrific for baking scones and cakes.

The skimmed milk left over at the beginning of the process was fed to the pigs. But that's not the end of the story. After churning, the butter had to be washed until the water ran clear. Then the butter was worked (beaten) in a butter worker, salt added and the butter weighed into pounds and half pounds.

The flavour of the butter varied from farm to farm and season to season. The diet and the breed of cow made a difference. In the summer when the cows ate fresh grass, the butter would be a lovely golden yellow. In the winter when they ate hay it would be paler. Before the days of refrigeration, some of the butter was stored by putting extra salt in it and then storing it in earthenware pans. By the end of winter it could get pretty rancid – but that was helped by washing it again.

The Bread Oven

Lighting the bread oven was only done once a week. Gorse or sticks were piled high in the oven and lit. When they were reduced to ash the oven would be hot. But how could you tell when it is just the right temperature? Jean Phillips: "I'd put my fist in the oven and hold it there. If I could count to 24, then it was right. If not – well it was too hot!"

Feathering

Feathering poultry was a year-round job, but four or five days before Christmas all the women on the farms downed tools to concentrate on feathering and dressing the birds. Turkeys were not much in evidence until the late 1950's. Asked why one member figured that turkeys had a rather delicate disposition, she answered: "They would just start to mope and die."

And this is how you deal with a goose: "Pluck the feathers out with the grain, or the skin will rip. Light some meths in a low flat dish and swing the bird over the flame to singe all the hairs off. The trick is to keep the goose moving or it will burn."

After it has been gutted and cleaned the correct way to dress a goose is to put the gizzard on one wing and the liver and heart on the other. These are then skewered on, through the wings. Making the skewers was considered the man's job. A month before Christmas, the men gathered hazel sticks and made them into skewers, which would then be dried in a rack by the fire.

94

Glenys Pugh's geese at Plas-y-Gaer

The feathers from the geese would be sold to make down for pillows and eiderdowns. Feathers were left on the wings, which were much prized as brushes. They would sweep up cobwebs or get into crevices that nothing else could reach.

The Pig

Every family had at least one pig, sometimes two or three. And the old saying that you could use every part of a pig except its squeak was absolutely true.

The pigs were well fed. Skimmed milk, barley, scraps, anything at all that was left over went to the pig. They were weighed by the score. A score equals twenty pounds or about 9 kilograms and a 'tidy' pig would weigh a good twenty score! One farmer is quoted as saying: "You know the pig is fat enough when it can't stand up." But those were the days when people liked fatty pigs. The fat might have been cooked off but it added hugely to the flavour."

Interestingly, Dr Arwyn Davies, a Brecon GP who specialised in cardiology at Brecon War Memorial Hospital, remarked on how few heart problems there used to be in a community which consumed such a large amount of fat bacon. He put this phenomenon down to the incredible amount of hard physical work, which kept the farmers and their families lean and fit. "You hardly ever see old photographs of fat farmers," he said.

Killing the pig and ensuring none of it was wasted involved a huge amount of work. A slaughterer would go from farm to farm to kill the pig. Then the job of making sure each part of the animal was used properly began. Water was heated in big boilers to scald the skin so the hairs could be scraped off. The favourite implement for this was the bottom of an old-fashioned candlestick. And there is a knack to that too – 'Steady and quick'.

The farm pig has just been killed at Pencaefadog
Dan Jones, Ted Davies, Jim Williams, Penry Davies, Tommy Davies,
Penry John Davies, Tim Price

Another way of getting rid of the hair was to put the pig onto a piece of zinc, surround it with bracken and burn it. Though this was a lot messier it gave a wonderful flavour to the crackling. Next came the job of gutting and cleaning the pig. Care had to be taken not to break the gall bladder, which could make the meat bitter. For two days the pig was hung to cool before being cut up. Lard would be taken to make scratchings. The intestines went to make chitterlings, the offal was turned into faggots and the head was used for brawn.

The spare ribs, griskin, chines and backbone were cut out and cooked and eaten immediately. They are not suitable for curing as bacon or ham and in the days before refrigeration, the custom was to share these choice pieces amongst family and neighbours. In turn you would receive some in return when they killed their pig. The rest of the pig would be salted and cured for bacon.

Eggs

Practically every home had a few chickens, but Hilda and Dennis Williams of the Twyn, Cantref, once had a thousand laying hens. Every evening when he finished work they had their meal and sat cleaning the eggs. This was all done with a kind of fine sandpaper. Because eggs are porous, washing them was not allowed. In the market hall in Brecon there used to be an egg packing station and a machine for sorting eggs into their various sizes.

Deliveries

One chore that is definitely a twentieth century creation is lugging bag-loads of shopping back from town or supermarket. WI members have fond memories of dropping off their order in town on market day and waiting for things to be delivered to the door. Groceries, bread, even a van selling work clothes all arrived on the doorstep.

The Week

Monday: Washing and scrubbing and hanging clothes to dry.

Tuesday: Ironing with flat irons heated on the stove. The men went to the Livestock Market in Brecon.

Wednesday: Cleaning, making butter and kneading dough for bread.

Thursday: Bread-oven lit and enough bread baked to last a week.

Friday: Market day. But before the women could buy anything, first they had to sell their produce – vegetables, butter, dressed chickens, rabbits, flowers, herbs from the garden. Farmers' wives were not given housekeeping money. They had to earn it by selling what they grew and made. Jean Phillips remembers picking mint and other herbs to sell in order to buy newspapers.

Saturday: Vegetables peeled, puddings and all food prepared for Sunday and the house cleaned ready for Sunday.

Sunday: Strictly observed as a day of rest and worship.

Vanished – Dinas

Tennis on the lawn at Dinas – May Day 1908
Now under the Brecon By-Pass

When John Lloyd (the Poet) of Dinas died in 1875, the Brecon County Times described him as a "Vigorous and racy specimen of the Welsh Country Gentleman". The memoriam went on, "He was extremely fond of all sports, of being out on the breezy mountains and of wandering the riverside. For many years he farmed extensively, and was a practical stock-breeder, with much success. He possessed considerable estates in Herefordshire, Monmouthshire and his own county."

In 1820, John Lloyd began work on building Dinas as a home for his family on the Abercynrig Estate, which his father had bought from Lord Ashbrook. In the study there, John Lloyd's great-grandson (also John), opened a letter from Neville Chamberlain asking him to accept a knighthood. In August 1926, Dinas was the setting for the 21st birthday party of Sir John's son Conway, a rising star in the Royal Navy.

In 1937, Conway married a beautiful American, Marie McRae Smith. Tragedy struck in 1939. Conway was aboard the submarine HMS Thetis, which sank with the loss of 99 lives. There were only four survivors, but John was not amongst them. Marie was pregnant and shortly afterwards her daughter, Anne-Marie, was born and Marie decided to return to America.

Conway Lloyd's 21ˢᵗ birthday party at Dinas August 1926

Sir John and Lady Lloyd were to face more dreadful news when their third son, John, who flew Hurricanes, was killed in action in 1940. In 1941 Dinas was requisitioned by the Army to be used to house an Indian Medical Unit. When the war ended Dinas was converted into flats.

Eventually it fell into disrepair, was demolished and today lies directly under the route of the Brecon by-pass. Sir John's second son Bill, who lived in Abercynrig, used to enjoy telling people, "I just drove through the Dinas dining room at 100 miles an hour!"

But Conway and Marie's baby daughter, Anne-Marie, was not lost to Wales and always enjoyed visits to Abercynrig. It's a strong bond that was sealed when Anne-Marie was eight years old. "That summer I spent with my grandparents at Abercynrig planted the seeds of my love for Wales. I got a clear understanding of how much Grandpa cared about Wales, the Usk Valley, the Beacons, all of it. It went from his insides to my insides and has stayed with me all my life. I will always see Wales as a special, beautiful place and the home of my fathers."

In 1995, she restored the old Dinas Lodge and now she and her husband John Caple spend two months in the Brecon Beacons every summer.

Leslie the Mill and Comrades
Still Flying High!

Leslie Williams (Leslie the Mill) is one of eight children, the third generation of the family to live at Abercynrig Mill, Llanfrynach, to which his grandparents moved in 1892. He celebrated his 91st birthday in 2010 and looks back on life as a milkman, working farmer, service with the RAF, broadcaster, author, magistrate and historian.

At the outbreak of the Second World War, Leslie joined the RAF and flew more than 30 missions with Bomber Command. It was while he was based at Abingdon in Oxfordshire that he met an attractive young woman called Joyce who was working in Intelligence.

Joyce remembers, "I used to see the unemployed Welsh miners in Oxford looking for work at Morris Cowley – but I didn't really know any Welsh people." She was to spend the rest of her life getting to know the Welsh! Leslie brought Joyce back to the Mill in 1946.

Coming from a comparatively sophisticated Oxfordshire to the Mill was a huge adjustment. Joyce had only visited it for half a day before arriving in time to face the legendary winter of 1947. There was no hot water and no electricity. Joyce was glad of the big fires, which "Kept the front of you warm and left your back very cold." Joyce says she did wonder if she needed her head looked at!

But 65 years later, Leslie and Joyce are still there after a lifetime involved in the local community. Joyce was present at the first meeting of Llanfrynach and Cantref Women's Institute in 1949 – an organisation that has proved a boon to many newcomers.

Leslie farmed full time, but spread his wings to become a familiar voice on the BBC, where he had a regular slot talking about farming matters. He was a Nuffield Farming Scholar and served on the boards of the Royal Welsh Agricultural Society and of Brecon Agricultural Society, about which he wrote a history called 'The Guiding Light' to celebrate its 250th anniversary in 2005.

Amongst many other roles, Leslie was a long serving magistrate. When 'Mr Stipendiary Williams' retired from the Brecon Bench, he was described as "Having a quick and inquiring mind, a no-nonsense approach to those who sought to disobey the court, and who was compassionate to those who had fallen on hard times."

Abercynrig Mill is on the Abercynrig Estate and Leslie has been closely associated with it and the Lloyd family all his life. Richard Lloyd, Abercynrig's most recent resident, says that whenever he has a question about anything concerning its running, it's the indispensable Leslie to whom he turns first.

In January 2011, Leslie talked to the Women's Institute about Llanfrynach in days gone by - memories which many of them shared. He has recorded in great detail a huge amount of local history and his contributions pop up throughout this book.

One familiar face at the Mill is Bernard Wright of Llanfrynach. While Leslie was flying with Bomber Command, Bernard, born in 1921, was flying with RAF Coastal Command in Sunderland flying-boats on convoy escort duties in the Western Approaches to the UK.

In 1969, Bernard's career as a Land Agent for the MOD brought him with his wife Mary and family to the Brecon area, a post he accepted without hesitation. Not surprising that Leslie and Bernard have a lot in common, not only stories from the war but also a love of the countryside and the Brecon Beacons in particular.

Leslie Williams (RAF Bomber Command) and his wife Joyce (RAF Intelligence, Bomber Command) welcome Bernard Wright (RAF Coastal Command).

BRECONSHIRE WAR AGRICULTURAL EXECUTIVE COMMITTEE.

HAMILTON HOUSE,
THE STRUET,
BRECON.

Date....................................

Preliminary Notice to Farmers in Regard to the
Ploughing Quota for the 1943 Harvest.

FARM........ *Drawsront* ....

PRESENT OCCUPIER .... *P. J. Davies* .... C.O. No. *B264*

DEAR SIR or MADAM,

I am directed to furnish you with the following preliminary particulars in regard to the area you are expected to plough and cultivate on the above-mentioned farm(s) for the 1943 harvest.

Total plough quota—not less than .... *80* ....acres.

of which not less than...... *16*............acres must be planted in wheat;

,, ,, ... *4* .... ,, ,, ,, potatoes.

You must seed down with grass and clover seeds not less than...... *12* ....acres in the Spring of 1943. A minimum of not less than...... *12* ....acres must be planted in drilled roots (this includes Kale but does **not** include potatoes).

The 1943 harvest will be of vital importance to this country and you are urged to do everything possible to produce bumper crops. Timely and thorough cultivations are essential.

Stubbles intended for roots and potatoes must be ploughed by 31st December, 1942; stubbles for cereals by 31st March, 1943; and land now in roots and potatoes by 30th April, 1943.

The Committee have the power to withhold the £2 per acre ploughing grant unless the ploughing and cultivations are carried out thoroughly and in time.

As a rule the best results with Autumn wheat are obtained from early sowing dates, especially on the uplands.

It is to be clearly understood that the responsibility for carrying out the order in time rests with the farmer—the fact that he has placed his order for ploughing, etc., with the Committee does not relieve him of this responsibility. The Committee cannot guarantee to carry out the work although they will do everything in their power to assist where it is felt that help is needed. Farmers with strong teams of horses especially **must** make full use of them so that the Committee can pay more attention to farms where implements, etc., are not available. An appeal is made to farmers with tractors to help their neighbours.

Appeals against the ploughing quota must be made within 7 days of the date of this notice.

The Committee feel certain that Breconshire farmers will do everything possible to make the 1943 harvest a record one.

Yours faithfully,

Executive Officer.

World War Two

Whilst farmers understood how important their work was in producing enough food for the nation, there is no doubt that one of the most unpopular of the wartime committees were the ones designed to tell farmers what to do.

Leslie Williams: "Each county selected a War Agricultural Executive Committee to order farmers to plough up areas of their farms and told them the acreage of potatoes, grain etc that they must grow.

"Farmers were not equipped to carry out this work, so there was a pool of machinery and tractor-drivers which were hired out. Some steep land was cultivated for the first time, something that many farmers disagreed with, and which earned the committee the nickname the 'Brains Trust'."

But the whole business did have its funny side. Leslie Williams tells this story: "One of the drivers, Ray Price, was very popular, young and game for anything. When he was working at the Werns at Llanbrynean, he unearthed a piece of chain which he thought would be useful, so he hitched it to his tractor and away he went – only to be surprised by water all around him – he had drained the canal which ran alongside!"

The Land Army arrived: girls and women from all over the country, many who had never been in the country before. Jean Phillips says: "It was amazing how they adapted. There were also lots of evacuees. So many came that the Village Hall was used to house classrooms. Some of the teachers came with them. A few gradually went back, but there are still some in the area who stayed and eventually married."

Emlyn Williams was working at Upper Chapel when he joined the Home Guard – but didn't like it much. "After a day's ploughing you'd have to go up onto the Epynt and spend the night in a dug-out watching for lights – then back to work on the farm the next day with hardly any sleep. And he didn't like the training: "Mostly at Cwm Gwdi where we practiced throwing grenades."

But others rather enjoyed their time in 'Dad's Army'. Dennis Williams and Ivor Phillips, Tylebrythos, were just two who turned up to practice in Llanfrynach Village Hall under the supervision of Lord Brecon. Their duties included guarding the Lock and watching the Canal Bridge as the canal was used for ferrying ammunition to the factories.

Llanfrynach Home Guard

Back row: Dennis Williams, Emlyn Williams, Trevor Davies, Austin Morgan. Middle row: Bert Parry, ?, Bernie Price, ?, ?, Tommy Morgan, Tim Price. Front row: Nobby Clarke, Fred Jones, Jackie Walters, Major Evans, Jack Phillips, Fred Vaughan, Dai Evans.

Bill Powell, the former caretaker of Llanfrynach Village Hall, remembers in 1942-3 large numbers of German prisoners of war working under armed guard to dig trenches for pipes from near the White Swan to get water to Glan Usk. German and Italian prisoners of war also worked on the farms and some of them settled in the area after the war, marrying local girls.

In 1942 there was a mock invasion held in Cantref in preparation for the Burma front and hundreds of Indians with their pack-mules came through the Gap Road. Mary Owen-Lowe (née Phillips) remembers they caused great excitement at her home, Pontbren Farm, where they camped for several nights. She sold milk to the Indians, who cooked their chapattis on camp-fires in the fields.

Though many men were exempt from military service because of the importance of food production, most families did have someone who was called up. Leslie Williams was one of seven brothers; three joined the army and one the navy, while he went into the RAF.

Leslie says he was acutely aware of how little the war seemed to impact on life in the countryside he had left. " I don't think many people in the area had any conception of the war – the death and destruction. "I remember flying over the village one Sunday as the congregation was coming out of church – it seemed to me as if time had stood still – nothing seemed to have changed."

Even the problems caused by rationing were seen as an opportunity by people with easy access to fresh produce. Mary Jones (née Davies), who lived with her husband Dan at Trosnant Cottage, remembered her mother churning butter and exchanging it for tea and sugar with a woman who came all the way from Merthyr Tydfil every week.

Glyn Owen-Lowe recalls: "Milk was collected off the farms in milk churns – though when the churns were delivered they often contained produce other than milk for the respected citizens of the South Wales Valleys."

After the War

Kate Williams, Highgrove Farm.
(From a project she wrote when she was 10)

Rationing went on for years after the war, because the whole of Europe was run down, and it took quite a long time for farmers to build up their production. The government was advising the farmers on technical improvements such as new chemicals and fertilisers.

The government also gave subsidy money to encourage more production. This approach was so successful that by the 1970s the country could feed itself from home produced food! In fact it was too successful because too much food became a problem because the prices went down. This is still a problem for farmers today, but the housewife has benefited from cheap food since the 1970s.

Emlyn Williams

Emlyn Williams celebrated his 93rd birthday in 2010. He always enjoyed farm work, particularly working with cows. As a child he loved cutting out pictures of cows from magazines and papers.

He grew up with his brother Dennis and sister Dora at Forest Gwendwr Farm at Gwendwr, near Builth. He left aged fourteen, and started work at Bryn Gago Farm, Upper Chapel, where he was paid £5.10s for five months work: "Not a lot of money even then…". He stayed at Bryn Gago for eighteen months. And then he made the first of several moves by taking himself to the hiring fair in Brecon.

Emlyn said that the custom was for the farmer, the night before the fair, to ask each farm hand if he wanted to go or stay. So when he wanted a change of scene, Emlyn took himself off to the hiring fair. He described how the top of Ship Street, Brecon, would be impassable for the crowd of men and women wanting jobs and farmers wanting workers; either men for the farms or women as maids.

The custom was for the farmer to offer half-a-crown to a potential worker – who would then refuse or accept it. This half-crown Emlyn called an 'earn'. If the 'earn' was accepted, then that was taken as a contact of employment until the next hiring fair.

After Bryn Gago he was taken on at the hiring fair to work at Blaen Cae Fawr, Merthy Cynog. A year later the farm was taken over to become part of the military range at Sennybridge. Once again Emlyn went to the hiring fair and this time he took at job at Felindre, Upper Chapel, working for Richard Davies and his nephew Abraham Moses.

It was while he was at Felindre that Emlyn's parents, Arthur and Sarah Williams, moved from the Loggin, Upper Chapel, to work with Billy Price at Upper Cantref Farm. A year later Emlyn decided to try for work nearer them and this time he left the hiring fair with a job at Tŷ Fry Farm, Llanfrynach, where he stayed for five years. But he still had itchy feet. So off to the fair again. This time he went to work for Jack and Dai Morgan at Pant y Cored, Garthbrengy for a year.

In 1949, for what was to be the last time, he made his way to the fair where he met John Price who farmed Tregaer, Llanfrynach. Mr Price duly offered Emlyn the half-crown 'earn', which, along with a promise of £30 for 6 months working as a cowman and farm worker, was accepted.

Emlyn is still there more than 50 years later; he has never retired and aged 93 he still thinks of himself as a working man. "Never retire – keep going if you can," is his philosophy. But why, when he came to Tregaer, did he decide his wandering days were over? The answer is simple: "The work was right – I liked working with cows." To start we had 16 cows and calves and 600 sheep. Eventually we had 1500 sheep and 38 cows and a bull.

Gwynne Griffiths with Emlyn Williams at Tregaer
They had been ear–marking lambs

John Price was an uncle to Gwynne Griffiths, who eventually took over Tregaer as a tied (rented) farm from the Maesderwen Estate. Emlyn continued working as a cowman. The days were long but satisfying, starting at 7am with milking to be done before a proper cooked breakfast, then cleaning out – by hand with a shovel.

Gwynne married Joyce Bufton and they had three children: John, Sally and Richard. Emlyn was a fixture in their childhood and he says of them, "I was happy here. They are a nice family and Joyce is a good cook – which helps."

But there was also time for friends, and every Sunday afternoon would find Emlyn visiting Penry and Dilys Davies at Caerau, and every Christmas he spent a day there feathering turkeys.

Emlyn riding Tracey, with Sooty the dog

Sally Griffiths remembers him arriving home covered in feathers and with a Christmas turkey in his hand. She described how Emlyn really was part of the family, living in the house with them. His bedroom was opposite hers, and every night there was a quiet knock and a "Goodnight" from Emlyn.

Hill farming breeds characters, and like everyone else, Emlyn remembers Dick Tyle Llwyd and in particular Dick's sister Bessie, who moved from Bailea to live in Magpie Cottage, Llanfrynach, where Emlyn lives today. She gave part of her garden there to become the Public Conveniences and Emlyn says how much he admires the team of volunteers who have recently taken on the job of cleaning them up and keeping them open. "Much nicer today than they have been for years," Emlyn says.

And as for that little boy Richard, who has become a hugely successful international businessman and who still regularly returns to Tregaer and considers Emlyn as "One of us" – Emlyn says, "Credit to him, he's not big-headed with it" – a quiet compliment from a lovely old-fashioned, decent man.

In 1994 Emlyn was awarded the Queen's Medal for long service with one farmer, which he received from the Princess Royal at the Royal Welsh Show.

Hiring Fairs

Hiring fairs began at a time of a serious national shortage of labour after the Black Death, when Edward III tried to regulate the labour market with the Statute of Labourers in 1351. Fairs became the major place for people to look for work and for employers to find the right person to fill the job.

Men and women looking for jobs would gather in the street or market place, often sporting some sort of badge or tool to denote their speciality, shepherds held a crook or a tuft of wool, cowmen brought wisps of straw, dairymaids carried a milking stool or pail and housemaids held brooms or mops, which is why some hiring fairs were known as mop fairs.

Employers would look them over and, if they were thought fit, hire them for the coming year, handing over a coin to seal the arrangement – what Emlyn Williams described as 'the earn'.

Women and girls as young as 14 came seeking jobs, and in Brecon they too had to stand around in the street, waiting to be chosen. But in 1890 a group of concerned citizens decided something should be done. This is from the forerunner to the Brecon and Radnor Express:

The Brecknock Beacon, May 1st 1891:

"…it was a relic of earlier and more barbarous times, that whilst on the first fair day Glamorgan Street and Wheat Street were crowded and thronged by cattle for sale, on the next day, young women and girls of respectable character and parentage, stood for many weary hours on the top of Ship Street, waiting to be hired. Through heat or rain, jostled and crushed by the passing crowds, within hearing of coarse jokes and bad or improper language, there they stood until they met with an employer who engaged them."

The Vicar of Brecon and a committee of ladies asked the Mayor, Cllr Morgan to help. He ordered that the hiring fair for girls should be moved to the Guild Hall where a comfortable warm room should be made available for the hiring of servant girls and each morning a competant registrar would take down the names of the girls looking for work and the places available.

The Brecknock Beacon approved: "We look to the Brecknockshire farmers and their wives to support a movement which will tend to surround the young women of Brecknockshire with more human influences, and remove them from conditions so unsuitable to their sex."

In the late 1950s, Margaret Sommers was a tax officer and remembers how busy the staff were on fair days. "Farmers would come to the 'Pay as you earn' department to find out how much tax they needed to deduct from the wages of the men. Farm workers did not fall into the ordinary tax system because they were paid their wages at the end of the complete six months. We often suspected that they would have been given some money before then, but as long as the correct tax was paid we were not worried!

Photograph from The Journal of Mary Gwladys Charles by Dr A. Gareth Jones
Two children at the 'Turnabout' Brecon Fair 1898

For children in the countryside and villages as well as in the town, fairs meant fun, and local schools had a half-day holiday. Margaret says the townsfolk would go to the fair on Monday evening or on Wednesday. "But Tuesday Fair Day was when all the country folk came to town." Traditionally the Tuesday Fair Day in November was when country people would bring a live pig to the market to be sold for bacon. The money from the sale of the pig would buy food for the winter. The pig would often be taken away and killed the same day.

Amusements occupied the whole of the town centre and the Market Hall was crowded with 'cheap jacks' selling their wares. Margaret remembers that in the 1940s there were still boxing booths at the fair - though as a child she was only allowedto go in the afternoon, for a ride on the merry-go-round, and when she was older, the Noah's Ark.

Photograph courtesy of the Clark family

Hiring Fair in Full Swing

Photograph courtesy of the Clark family

Crowds at the Boxing Booth at the Fair

Love at the Fair

One couple got more than they bargained for when they went looking for work at the Brecon Hiring Fair. Annie Phillips, who lived at Old Cwmcynwyn in Cantref in the 1880s, and David Benjamin Moses, a shepherd from Brynfedwyn Farm on the Penpont Estate, not only found jobs at Upper and Lower Cantref – but also met and found each other and were married in June 1906.

The wedding of Annie Phillips and Benjamin Moses 1906

Photograph courtesy of Brecknock Museum

One of the last hiring fairs to be held in Brecon
Just a few job-seekers at the top of Ship Street in the 1960s

112

"An Unforgivable Thing!"

The very real 'apartness' of Cantref and Llanfrynach is one of the great mysteries of local life. The country hill farming community that is Cantref, and the lowland farming village of Llanfrynach, are next-door neighbours. They share a Community Hall. They are friendly and polite to each other. But make no mistake, they are each proud and possessive about their own patch and their own community identity.

Jean Phillips – "did the unforgivable thing"
Born in Cantref – married a man from Llanfrynach!

It's a fact Jean Phillips has recognised all her life. "I was born at Upper Cantref in 1924. My one and only brother was born in 1932. My parents lived at Upper Cantref and my grandparents at Lower Cantref.

"I did the unforgivable thing and married a man from Llanfrynach, but we redeemed ourselves by buying Lower Cantref, where two of my children, John and Robert, were born.

"We moved down the road to Tŷ Fry, Llanfrynach, in 1951, when my father-in-law died, and once again Lower Cantref was sold. I have returned to Cantref, particularly to the church, throughout my life, and have happy memories and many good friends in both parishes."

There has always been speculation about why such small communities, so close together, have not merged into one. One theory is that Cantref really is a series of extended families – and even newcomers are quickly infected with wanting to be part of what might be described as the 'Cantref Tribe'.

Pity then the council official, who in 2006 looked at a map of the area and decided that Llanfrynach and Cantref could just as easily be served by the same community councillors. Easy to think the two wards could be merged when you see there are only about 70 adults on the electoral role in Cantref, and almost 300 in Llanfrynach. But Powys County Council had not understood the deep-rooted difference between village and country life.

Though they may live within a few miles of each other, the problems faced by hill farmers and residents of isolated homes are very different from those affecting residents of a village with pavements, street lighting and regular rubbish collections.

But there is also a big emotional difference, which is harder to define. Residents of Cantref can punch above their weight when roused and a short but fierce campaign ensued, in which every voter in Cantref and Nant Ddu signed a petition and wrote letters demanding their right to separate representation.

**Children of Cantref present their community's petition
to Powys County Councillor Dorothy James in 2006**

They won the fight and Cantref with Nant Ddu was allowed to continue as a separate ward and retain its two councillors on Llanfrynach Community Council (which also serves Groesffordd with Lechfaen and Llanhamlach).

When the Community is Family

The days when a huge extended family could all be found living within the same few square miles have almost vanished. But in Cantref, the old families: Phillips, Evans and Davies, all have descendants farming here today. With only 70 adults on the electoral role, these families make up most of it! They will also ensure the next generation is waiting to carry on farming the hills.

The Phillips Family

Talybont Christmas Market 1976
Ivor Phillips, John Davies (butcher), Bill Phillips, Dai Phillips, Llewellyn Richards

Three Phillips brothers in this photograph farmed neighbouring farms in Cantref. Ivor Phillips, Tylebrythos, Bill Phillips, Pontbren and Dai Phillips, The Neuadd.

The family can trace its local roots back for centuries, and Ivor, Bill and Dai were known far and wide as great farming characters – Gethin Havard from the British Wool Marketing Board recalls, "On the day Cantref brought its wool to the Board, the three of them, in long farming macs, walking from the Boars Head through town to the Market Tavern – was one of the great sights of those days." Their many grandchildren play a big part in farming in the Beacons today.

The Evans Family

The earliest record of the Evans family in Llanfrynach and Cantref is of Thomas Evans, born at Tir Ciw in 1761. He married Anne and they had four children. Ever since there have been Evans's in the community at Llwyncelyn, Plas-y-Gaer, Old Crofftau and now at New Croftau Farm.

One of the most loved and active members of the family was 'Aunty Peggy'. She was the eldest of 10 children, and grew up at Tir Ciw; she later lived at Wern-y-Marchog and Pwll. She was a real mother to the community, famous for being a help to anyone in difficulty, for turning her hand to everything, always there on shearing, threshing, and feathering days and at the end, laying out those who had passed away. In particular she loved Cantref Church and cleaned it regularly for as long as she was able.

Margaret Jane (Aunty Peggy) Evans
1882 – 1963

Her intelligence, capacity for hard work, and good nature have been passed on to the many Evans women who have made, and continue to make, a huge contribution to life in the Beacons.

116

Peggy's youngest brother Albert Edward (known as Dick) had four daughters: Glenys Pugh, June Matthews, Jean Williams and Mary Davies, and one son, Richard, known to everyone far and wide as Boyo. Glenys is a skilled needlewoman and has spent hours creating a beautiful altar cloth for Cantref Church where she was the People's Warden until 2009.

The Evans family is now spread to various corners of Wales, but Boyo's sons Howard and Aubrey and his grandchildren Robert and Shauna are growing up in the hill farming and community tradition.

Photograph Susan Brook

Robert Evans age 7 with friends at Libanus Show Cantref 2010

The Davies Family

If you find yourself at a party, a meeting or in a group of people working in Cantref, it would be impossible not to find yourself with several members of the Davies family. Five generations ago the Davies family was established at Tir-y-Groes, Cantref. In the years that followed, different branches of the family moved out to live at Trosnant, Pencaefadog, Berllan, The Wern and several other homes in Cantref.

Tir- y-Groes, Cantref - Early 1900s

Photograph Susan Brook

Some of the current generation of the Davies Family
Baden, Michelle, Sheila, David, Carol with Kim Brook

The Stephens Family

Photograph Susan Brook

Three Generations of Hill Farmers
Denzil Stephens with his grandsons Aneirin and Llywelyn and son Brychan
On top of Pen y Fan at the Walk to Worship 2007

Three generations of the Stephens family farm Cwmcynwyn and Bailea Farms just below the Hill Gate on the Gap Road. Compared to other families in Cantref they are relative newcomers having only arrived in 1950s! But there is no doubt they are hill farmers to their inner core.

Newcomers

With such strong family presences in the community the newcomer might think it would be impossible to feel at home here. But the reverse is true. And while no-one can quite become a member of someone else's family, in Cantref the locals have extended a warm welcome to the Chamberlains, Smiths, Williams's, Brooks and others who have settled in.

Sue and Graham Chamberlain are amongst this small group of newcomers to Cantref, and have thrown themselves into local life – to the point where at Libanus Show in Cefn Cantref they walked off with four prizes including first for a bale of meadow hay – the first they had ever grown.

Photograph Susan Brook

Sue and Graham Chamberlain, Cantref.

However, it turns out that Sue may not be such a newcomer as she first thought. Research into her family tree has revealed that her ancestors were living in the Brecon area since 1770. It was a particular thrill for her to discover that her great-grandparents lived in Old Cwmcynwyn, Cantref in 1886 – just a short way from where she lives today. *(See the story of how her grandparents met at a hiring fair p 112.)*
"It feels as if I have really come back to Where I Belong", she said.

Wind, Rain or Shine – The Weather

For this, as for every other farming community, the weather is all-important and inescapable. Come rain or shine the animals and the crops have to be tended. A fine season or a foul one can make all the difference between profit and loss.

Photograph Susan Brook

Cwm Sere in the Snow

It's quite common for neighbouring communities like Llanfrynach and Cantref to have different weather in spite of being only two or three miles apart. Because of the sharp increase in altitude it can be foggy in the village and clear on the hills and vice versa. Standing on the Beacons in the early morning and looking down at the sun shining on the mist swirling around below is reminiscent of the parts of old maps where land has yet to be explored and which carry the warning: 'Here Be Dragons'.

121

Everyone recalls the winters which had memorable snow: 1947, 1962/3, 1982 and 2010. Ivor Phillips said the snow was so deep during the winter of 1947 that they could not get the sheep through the hill gate, and men from the council came with their shovels to help. That winter the children did not go to school for six weeks.

It was a time that Austin Morgan, Tynllwyn, remembered for a visit he made through deep snow to one of the more remote farms in the area, Tyle Llwyd.

"My father told me 'Go and see Dick and his cousin Lewis. They could be dead up there and nobody would know.' When I got there Dick showed me all the ewes that were dead in the garden. Out of a flock of several hundred, just 29 had survived."

One of the reasons that so many sheep died that winter was that they had never learnt to eat hay – farmers usually left them to graze and to scrape away some snow to get at the grass. Austin Morgan said that when the snow of 1947 got too deep for the sheep to get through, hay was put out for them to eat. But they didn't know what it was for. They just walked over it and many starved to death.

The only way to get them to understand was to pen them tightly together with some loose hay, and after a couple of days they would eat it. But many hill farmers did not have the facilities to do this – their sheep ignored the hay that lay on the open ground, trying to eat bark of the trees instead. After this hard lesson, ewe lambs are now regularly fed hay at 12 months old as a matter of course.

Gwynne Griffiths of Tregaer cut ivy off the trees to feed the sheep in the very hard winters: "It may seem daft, but we did it and the sheep would come running when they heard the sound of the axe chopping down a tree for the ivy. The ivy seemed to stimulate their appetite. Sheep were even allowed to graze in the churchyards to get what grass they could. But it wasn't enough. Sheep huddled into the church porch for shelter and died there."

And after the snow melted came the floods, when even more sheep were drowned.

In the years between the first and second world wars the Lodge Pond (at Tŷ Mawr, Llanfrynach) was regularly frozen over. Leslie Williams remembers hundreds of people gathered there to skate. "Vivien Lewis (later Lord Brecon) provided lights from his car so people could continue to skate through the night. Even Llangorse Lake froze over sufficiently for a horse and cart to cross the lake."

Jean Phillips wrote: "There was a time in the late thirties when the Lodge Pond was frozen for thirteen weeks. In 1947 it was impossible to get a car out on the road from Cantref for six weeks. There were no gritters or snowploughs in those days."

Skating on the Lodge Pond, Tŷ Mawr, Llanfrynach

In fact everyone remembers the ice regularly being six inches or so thick on the Lodge Pond and also the ponds at Pencaefadog and Trosnant. Several local people still have their skates stored away in the attic!

High on the hills there are trees growing at alarming angles, bent by the prevailing winds from the West. Sometimes the wind on the Beacons is so strong you can almost lean on it. But when the sun shines, the skies are blue and the larks sing, it's hard to believe things can alter in a matter of minutes.

The only predictable thing about weather in the Brecon Beacons is that you never know when it can suddenly change. There are days when all the seasons of the year seem to happen in one day.

"Go out prepared" is always the advice from the Brecon Mountain Rescue Team. This group of volunteers is on call 24/7 to help those in difficulty and the number of times they have to turn out is increasing. The Mountain Rescue Team members are all volunteers, and they provide help not only to any mountain walkers and climbers who get into difficulties, but also local residents who may get trapped in isolated farms by snow and ice; sometimes the Mountain Rescue Team is the only emergency service that can reach them.

Brecon Mountain Rescue Team with the then Bishop of Swansea and Brecon, Rt. Rev Anthony Pierce, on top of Pen y Fan at the Walk to Worship in July 2007

One Woman's Weather

Libby Richards

**Libby Richards with Jim Eckley and Heindrich Josef Stübl (former German POW)
Gathering Ponies 1950s**

I was born just after the "tups were put out to the ewes on the hill". My one sister was born "just before shearing" and the other one was badly planned and arrived late during the lambing.

My memory of this time as a five-year-old was of wet nappies, wet Wellingtons and socks, wet dogs, wet orphan lambs, all competing for a position for warmth near the Aga in the large farm kitchen.

My life has always linked to the sheep, the hills and 'the wet'. Rain, rain, rain; and yet I am happy in the rain, it seems to suit my body. Is this adaptation to my environment? The same reason that the cry of a lamb awakes in me a quick response that a mother always gives at the sound of any baby's cry.

A hill-farming life, tuned to nature. We can plan, make provision for the long hard winter, cut the grass to be turned into hay by the sun in the summer, but we have learned to accept the unexpected. We have always failed to win against the force of Nature.

There is no way we can beat the cold lashing rain in May, that unexpected cruel East wind that dries up the ewes' milk and makes them abandon their lambs, the late snow that can sometimes arrive during the lambing, burying the ewes that have taken shelter against the hill wall.

Above all the summer sun always seems to elude us, so in many ways the black soggy stuff that was to have been the hay has also become part of the way of life. The weather, the sheep, the hills….

Winter: at this time of year the fog comes down. It is as if there is no longer a division between the earth and the sky, you are walking in the sky. The soft mist is in your hair, gentle against your face, enveloping your whole self, another world. A mysterious world, with loud sounds and distorted vision. A log on the ground can look like a body; an outcrop of rock becomes a castle from the fairy-tales of childhood.

Photograph Susan Brook

"no longer a division between the earth and the sky"

126

There is an inner fear; it is so easy to be lost, all the familiar landmarks erased. Suddenly a sheep, huge, like a large wild animal, appears in this wet enclosed world, only to quickly disappear, leaving you alone again, surrounded by cloud.

It is a time of great melancholy, the frantic time of the sales and sortings are over and the continuing winter with fierce storms has to be faced. It can be a lonely time, it can be a desperate time, people tied to the land, isolated on their farms, troubled by their inner disquiet, nowhere to turn.

The high incidence of depression and suicide in rural areas portrays this, just yourself, your responsibilities, no way out except with a gun. It seems rational, any animal that cannot cope with the rigours of life is 'put out of its misery' so it seems a logical step.

It is often at the end of winter, with the expectation of spring, when the birds start singing, the sap starts rising and everywhere there is new life and new hope, that the despair gets worse and the thought of another round of the farming year intensifies the loneliness within.

However it is not all gloom – as R. S. Thomas wrote:

"In these uplands we have people who enjoy life.
Neighbour to the wind and cloud and the wild birds of the moor…"

Photograph Brecon Beacons National Park Authority

And at the end of March the lambs begin to appear………

127

Harvest – Then and Now

These two photographs say it all. In the lifetime of the young girl standing in front of the haystack, the whole of farming has been changed by the mass production of the combustion engine.

That harvest scene, at Tir-y-Groes, Cantref, pictured in the 1940s, has changed almost beyond recognition. Betty's son, Revd David Thomas, remembers: "As a child I would see my grandfather and Jim Preece (who worked at Tir-y-Groes for 32 years) spend hours making corn ricks, hoeing swedes and ploughing with the old but dependable Ferguson T20. My mother, of course, remembers them using horses – Jolly and Flower.

"I remember sheaves of corn and stooking them and then turning them to dry. With the hay harvest I remember the small bales and my mother remembers hauling loose hay, which was a painstaking job."

This is how the harvest used to be, as told to Sheila Jarman at the WI reminiscence evening: "For centuries hay was cut by scythe and turned with a pikel to dry and brought on sledges to the barn. Corn was also cut by scythe and then tied with a few pieces of corn in sheaves and stacked until they dried enough to be stored in the barns.

When it was time to thresh the corn, the farmers would all help each other. The threshing machine, which separates the grain from the stalks, would come around each farm pulled by horses. Enough corn was grown to feed the animals and to keep seed for next year."

Leslie Williams says: "This work was much later in the year than today, and hauling corn at the time of the harvest moon was usual. Although no Luddite, I feel that the introduction of machinery destroyed the pride of manual labour – for instance when stooking sheaves of corn, the stooks had to be erected in straight lines like drill soldiers."

After the introduction of the engine, the first mechanised help was called a deliverer. Then came the binder and then the combine harvester and the round baler, which produces the huge rolled bales of hay, silage and straw we have today.

Harvest Home at Tir-y-Groes 1940s
Jim Preece, Betty Davies (now Thomas), Fred Williams, Jim Davies

Photograph Ivor Jay

Hay Bales at Bailea, Cantref.

Cattle

Welsh Black and Hereford are the breeds of cattle predominately associated with Wales and which are at the foundation of the Welsh beef industry today.

The Welsh Black is descended from cattle that roamed in the rough mountains and hill-country before the Romans arrived. They have been bred here for more than a thousand years and were often used as currency – hence the description of them as 'the black gold from the Welsh hills'.

Herefords as a breed came about in the 18th century and are a firm favourite with hill farmers here today. Austin Morgan, born at Tynllwyn in 1926, grew up to become one of the country's foremost breeders and a judge of both Hereford cattle and Texel sheep. In 1995 he was President of Brecon Show.

Today, cross-breeding with continental breeds such as Limousin and Charolais has created cattle with better conformation for the modern meat market.

**Austin Morgan with Horsetin I. "Rotorua" – a polled Hereford
Sold at Edinburgh Sales in 1981 for 3,500 guineas**

Dairy Cattle

Milking the cow used to be a daily chore for many of the people who have contributed to this book. Today milk is imported from abroad and often sold as a loss-leader in supermarkets. The dairy industry is in crisis, with first-class dairy-farmers no longer able to make enough to live on.

Cefn Cantref was home to one of the finest herds of dairy cattle in Wales. Brian Williams and his wife Stephanie worked hard to build up their herd of Holstein Friesians and won many prizes with their stock. When their son Mathew went to agricultural college in 1995, he was confident about his future in farming.

But at the beginning of the millennium the crisis in dairy-farming meant the family's dairy cattle and bull calves were worth very little. Mathew was heartbroken when he recorded, "The value of the cows is practically nothing and I've just had to take another batch of dairy bull calves to the hunt kennels in Brecon to be shot and fed to the hounds." In the Spring of 2000, Matthew was one of thirty-five Welsh milk producers who poured milk on their land to draw attention to the crisis facing them.

A Desperate Protest
Mathew Williams pours his milk onto the land

Within a couple of years the Williams family had decided to get out of farming altogether. They left Cefn Cantref and Brian became a qualified homeopath – he had become interested in treating his cattle with homeopathic remedies and now has a flourishing practice in Brecon and Glasbury.

The Shearing Shed, Pontbrengarreg, Cantref, 1973

Back: Tom Phillips, John Hooper, Ivor Davies, David Davies, Terry Owen-Lowe, Bill Phillips, Ivor Phillips, Tommy Davies, David Phillips,

Front: Ray Phillips, Graham Davies, Harry Badham, Fred Jones.

Edgar Powell, Dai Phillips.

Sheep

Photograph Garfield Kennedy

Welsh Mountain Sheep (Defaid Mynydd Cymreig) at Bailea, Cantref

Not surprisingly, the most common sheep here are white Welsh Mountain sheep, the Brecknock Hill breed. They have no wool on the face or legs, and they have long tails, which are normally left undocked.

Other common varieties are the Badger-Face Welsh Mountain, which comes in two varieties, white with a dark face and belly, and black with a white belly and white stripes over the eyes.

Balwen Welsh Mountain are black, but go brown in the sunlight and grey with age.

Black Welsh Mountain sheep are just that – black. There are often one or two black sheep in a flock but they are also bred as a separate variety. Libby Richards *(see her family's story on pages 41-45)* points out that "An odd black sheep or unusually marked sheep is sometimes kept in order to make the recognition of a certain group easier."

South Wales Mountain sheep are larger than other Welsh Mountain breeds. They are white with tan markings on their legs and face, with a brown collar.

The Festival of the Year – Shearing

Libby Richards

My memories of helping at shearing go back a long way. The noise of the constantly bleating sheep, the barking dogs, the shouting on the yards and then the dark cool interior of the barn, the snip, snip of the shearing blades, the smell of the wool mingling with that of pipe tobacco, the shouting "Pitcho!" and the running child with the pitch pot. This was just after the Second World War. To go back further, I interviewed two people who had taken part in shearings during the time of my grandparents.

Mary Seabrook (née Davies) was born in 1914. She told me: "We started preparing for shearing the week before, picking gooseberries and rhubarb from the garden to make tarts. Dry goods were ordered to be delivered by pony and trap. Blaentaf was the hill farm where the shearing took place, being the home of the shepherd and his family. Thirty men slept in the loft. Mattress covers were stuffed with straw for their beds and blankets were stored in a coffer for their use.

"All the table cloths, cutlery and pots and pans were kept in the far room and only brought out for shearing. The big range and baking oven were ready, huge rice puddings and tarts and cakes were cooked. A sheep was killed every day. Eighty men were fed at long trestle tables.

The men ate in two shifts. Breakfast was boiled fat bacon, bread and cheese, with mugs of tea. Lunch was mutton and mint sauce, cabbage, peas, potatoes and gravy. Then fruit-tart or rice-pudding. Tea was bread and butter and fruitcake and a mug of tea. Supper was cold meat and salad, bread and butter, and cold rice-pudding.

We washed the tablecloth every night, together with the towels that the men had used after washing their hands in the big tin bath outside the porch on their way in for food. We used to go for walks in the evening with the young men, but your grandparents didn't like it. They never wanted anybody to get married. We would end the evening sitting by the fire telling stories.

There was a man whom we used to call Shoni Shimla (this is from the Welsh "simnai" meaning chimney) who was a very good ventriloquist and used to throw his voice up the chimney. He was a roadster, or tramp, with no proper home; he used to appear for every shearing to do odd jobs and enjoy the company and the good food.

A group outside the barn at Blaentaf on Shearing Day 1921
Shoni Shimla is the man with a moustache, nearest the tree and the young boys

He had a withered hand and used to scare us when it was dark by throwing his voice and running this deformed hand through our hair. His real name was Bill Phillips, no-one knew where he came from but shearing would not have been the same without him."

Shearing Today

Today the job of shearing is a lot easier, with new methods and equipment. When the job was done by hand, it took, on average, an hour to shear a dozen sheep. These days with electric clippers the men can shear thirty or more sheep in an hour – though with hundreds of sheep on each farm, shearing is still a massive task and next to lambing the big event of the hill farming calendar. Sheep-shearing is a great way for young farmers to see the world. They can travel with the shearing seasons, getting work in Australia, New Zealand, the Falkland Islands, South America, North America, Britain and then over to Norway.

Photograph Susan Brook

Shearing a Sheep at Libanus Show, Cefn Cantref 2010

It has also become a fiercely-fought competition scene, with the World Championships in 2010 happening at the Royal Welsh Show. And it all begins at local level. Even Libanus Show in Cantref has young farmers vying for prizes.

On Tack

Because of the treacherous weather in the hills each winter, many sheep are taken to a milder climate. Half the cost of this is paid to the lowland farmer when the sheep arrive and the remainder when they are collected. If any die they are not paid for. An old custom was that the ears of the dead lamb were kept as evidence, to prove that the lamb had not been sold.

One job that is not done at all these days is washing the sheep before they are sheared, a practice that came to an end in the 1960s, by which time the effort was no longer worth it. One bitterly cold memory for Emlyn Williams came in midsummer – the time when sheep had to be washed. He was working at Felindre Farm, Upper Chapel, where the job was done in a big pool. As the youngest worker on the farm it was Emlyn who had to get in the water with the sheep. And though the day was warm the water was freezing. When he got out half-an-hour later, he was rewarded with a stiff tot of whisky.

The Wool

Today the word 'fleece' describes something made of polyester, which bears no relation at all to anything a sheep would recognise! The use of wool, once a staple of daily life, declined dramatically with the introduction of modern fibre and the fashion for wooden and tile floors rather than carpet.

Prices fell so low that the money for a wool fleece did not cover the cost of shearing the sheep, though of course the job still has to be done for the well-being of the animals. But by 2010, prices had begun to improve and the Prince of Wales, as patron of the Campaign for Wool, is backing the movement to bring wool back into fashion. Hearing of plans for new breeds of sheep that lose their wool naturally, to be brought in as a cost-cutting measure, he said: "That seems to me to be the absolute epitome of all that is wrong in the way that we look at the world."

After shearing, each farmer has an appointment to take all the rolled fleeces to the Wool Marketing Board in Brecon. In a tradition unique to Cantref, a whole day is set aside for the farmers to bring in their wool. This used to be another great community occasion, with Fred Ackroyd, the manager, and the farmers all retiring to the Boar's Head afterwards.

Hopefully the huge benefits of wool for a wide variety of uses, from making mattresses for babies to insulating houses, as well as by the fashion industry, will create a new market for this most natural of products.

Lambs

But it's lambing which is the most magical as well as the most exhausting time of year for sheep farmers. Until relatively recently, lambing happened outdoors in all weathers. But today, on most farms, huge sheds provide shelter and warmth for both sheep and farmers. The first lambs appear in lowland fields shortly after Christmas. But lambing gets later and later the higher up the Beacons you go, until at about 1000 ft, it's March or even April, when the worst of the weather is past, that the bouncing spring crop arrives.

Many strangers to the countryside don't realize it's the male lambs that become much-prized Welsh spring lamb. Hill lambs are weaned from their mothers every August. Most male lambs go for slaughter, but the ewe-lambs are kept for breeding in the autumn of the following year.

Terry Owen-Lowe
Lambing Time at
Pontbrengarreg, Cantref
1995

Most of the sheep and cattle are sold in the local markets at Brecon, Sennybridge, Talybont or Talgarth. The lambs are weighed and graded and the fat lambs go for slaughter for the food chain. The store lambs (those not fat enough to kill) are sold on to fatten.

Rams

To avoid interbreeding, fresh rams are needed on each farm every year. So in September, farmers congregate at the Ram Sales at Talybont-on-Usk, Sennybridge and Builth Wells. Some farmers even go up to the huge Ram Sale at Lockerbie in Scotland to buy rams.

Fresh rams arrive at New Croftau Farm

So what makes a good ram? Libby Richards: "A Welsh Mountain ram must have good confirmation: a good character head, traditionally with horns, a long body with well-fleshed hindquarters, set squarely on four strong legs: the cry of the auctioneer, "Look at the timber under him" means just this."

Dipping

Dipping sheep to prevent external parasites, especially scab-mite, has long been a controversial issue. For many years, farmers used DDT, arsenic or OP dips to do the job. But these undoubtedly had a harmful effect on the environment and, many believe, on the farmers themselves.

Many are convinced they have suffered ill-effects. Painful and aching limbs, tiredness, acute depression, even suicide: all these and more have been laid at the door of chemicals that farmers were forced by law to use.

Because the eradication of scab and other parasites was considered vital, the dipping of sheep in these chemicals became a legal requirement. In 1970, the Weights and Measures Department, (succeeded by the Trading Standards Department), became responsible for enforcing a law for which many farmers think they paid a high price. Police officers used to go round the farms to inspect every dipping and to ensure each sheep was totally immersed in the dip for 30 seconds. Today these chemicals are no longer in use.

Dipping sheep – under the watchful eye of the law

Shepherds – A Rare Breed

Knights of the Mountain
Jim Eckley, Rickie Evans, Walter Eckley, David Eckley

Shepherds who earned the respect and affection of the whole farming community were Walter, James and David Eckley. James, the eldest, was born in 1874 and died at the age of 95. He worked for many years at Cwm Oergwm, while David and Walter were shepherds for the Richards family at Abercriban Farm and then at Pwllycalch Farm. Jim's son Ray, who lives in Llanfrynach, describes them as "Knights of the mountain".

These men, who each started shepherding on the Beacons at the age of 13, were described by the Brecon and Radnor Express in 1954 as "Tough, weather-beaten farmers who know the dangers of the mountain mists and the dread of the heavy snowstorms which threaten the lives of their flocks".

As a mark of their regard for the contribution the Eckleys made to life on the Beacons, their fellow shepherds presented them with crooks and a citation which said, "For their many acts of kindness to people and animals that came their way. Due to their very high standard of hill-shepherding and unselfish neighbourly actions, many have benefited."

Ron Healey, born in Brecon in 1937, worked as a shepherd at Cwm Oergwm for Henry Pugh and at Pentwyn for Donald Jones, the last farmer to be seen regularly shepherding on horseback until his death in 1998. However, some farmers, like Dai Davies Pencaefadog and Jill Evans New Croftau, still enjoy taking part in the gathering on horseback.

Now in his 70s, Ron still works for Donald's son Thomas, and in 2011 the Buckland Manor Graziers Association plans to present him with a painting of a sheepdog to say thank you for all the work he has done on the hills and local farms since he started as a young boy many years ago.

Thomas said, "Ron is the last real shepherd in this area, and the day he retires will be the end of a great tradition. I hope he will carry on for some time yet."

Ron Healey
Fifty years as a shepherd on the Beacons

Jill Evans, New Crofftau Farm, riding Huw on Allt Ddu

David Davies, Pencaefadog, on Scarlet

From the sunshine and into the shadows below Cribyn
The sheep come through the Gap and down the hill

Running down Bryn Teg towards the Hill Gate and home to Cwmcynwyn

Gathering

The Duke of York marching his men up and down the hill has nothing on the farmers of the Brecon Beacons, who have to get the sheep up and down the mountains several times each year.

To gather the sheep and bring them down from the hills, farmers and their dogs are strategically placed on the hillside to form a cordon to ensure that no sheep escape, and they are all driven forward. Ron Healey says it is like a military operation.

The sound of farmers whistling and shouting commands to sheep, dogs and each other is reminiscent of the Wild West. The sight of sheep suddenly arriving at the crest of one of the hills, or in the 'V' of the Gap Road, and then pouring over the land below, has been described as "Like watching milk spill on the Beacons". It is a dramatic picture.

By and large, the sheep seem to go down to the right hill gate to get home to their farm – each lamb following its mother and learning the way. This is a hefted flock, developed over generations of breeding on the hills to know their "cynefin" – "where they belong". But there are always some strays, many of which end up at the Neuadd, from where the owners collect them. John Phillips, the Neuadd, knows all the earmarks for miles around.

Dogs

The shepherd's greatest asset, and often one of his greatest friends, is his dog. It would be impossible to farm hill sheep without them. From the start man has used dogs to help with shepherding by exploiting the dog's instinct for rounding up animals. Their earliest use was to guard the flock against wild animals.

A hill dog needs huge stamina, as described by Thomas Firbank in his book, I Bought a Mountain: "Our mountain dogs are quite different from the trials breed. A mountain dog must have tremendous vigour, for sheep do not wait for him to approach. They begin to move away as soon as someone appears on the skyline, and a dog must cover half a mile of rough country to overtake and retrieve them…"

Libby Richards: "There is no-one more sensitive than a shepherd about his dog's behaviour. It can only be compared to the hurt a parent feels over the criticism of their child: defending quickly, with a mixture of love and responsibility. Many a friendship has been tested at the end of a hill gathering if it is pointed out that a dog has performed badly and "Let a bunch of sheep go back".

Ron Healey reckons it takes about four years to "Teach a dog a bit of everything". Ron has trained and enjoyed working with many dogs, but he remembers a few in particular: "I had a lovely bitch called Queenie. In my eyes she could talk. Then there was Wallace. When we were gathering he would run all the way down the flank side of the flock like a winger in a football match. He knew exactly what he was doing. Monty on the other hand was a good driving dog."

So how did he train them? Or do sheepdogs teach each other? Ron says: "No, I don't let them run together. I reckon they've got to learn to use their own brains. When you call "Meg!" It's got to be Meg that comes, not one of the other dogs. My wife Betty starts training them when they're pups, takes them for walks, teaches them not to follow cars. You see, first you've got to teach a dog to listen."

Training a sheepdog properly may take years, but it can pay dividends. A well-trained sheep dog can easily sell for a thousand pounds or more.

Photograph Tracey Evans

Aubrey Evans' dog Meg and her mum Nell.

Fire–Break
The Foot and Mouth Crisis in the Beacons
Susan Brook

There are some words in every language that are so much a part of the soul of the people that their full meaning can never quite be translated. In Welsh one of those words is 'cynefin'. It is used in the title of this book to mean 'belonging' and it does. But Cynefin is belonging plus - it's belonging in the way a limb belongs to a body, part of how the whole body functions and is healthy.

When thousands of sheep, descended from stock grazed on the Beacons for generations, and unaffected by foot and mouth, were shot, the trauma was akin to amputating a healthy part of a healthy body. The revulsion was visceral, the grief unimaginable.

Photograph Janet Foster

In the early months of 2001, foot-and-mouth disease was headline news every night. All movement of animals everywhere had been brought to a halt. Prime Minister Tony Blair declared, "We are getting the disease under control" paving the way for the announcement of the election date on 3rd May. But between May and June foot-and-mouth continued to spread and one million animals were killed. By the time the crisis was over that figure had risen to six million animals, including four million sheep, across the UK.

In the Beacons, because of the movement restrictions, the sheep were all still down from the hills, in sheds and fields after the winter. Farmers were tense. Would the hill farms escape or not?

Disinfectant was used going in and out of all premises. Bio-security became all-important. Sheep were not allowed on the hill to graze and there was a shortage of fodder. Markets, where animals would normally be sold, were all closed, resulting in too much stock of all types going hungry on farms. It was decided that if the animals could not be fed they would be taken away for slaughter and the government would pay compensation under the Animal Welfare Scheme.

Suddenly the word came that the sheep would be allowed back on the hills. And hope began to rise - just a little. Little did the farmers know they would never bring these sheep home again.

Early in July 'Operation Beacon' had been set up by DEFRA to try to limit the effects of any proposed cull. Blood-tests were carried out to see if the disease had spread into any of the hefted flocks.

The year went on and it was time for shearing. This has to be done for the welfare of the animals, and usually the hill would have been gathered and the sheep sheared in sheds on the farms. This time, the farmers had to go onto the hills to shear their flocks. The wool was discarded and later collected and destroyed.

Ivor Davies, The Wern, and neighbours shearing sheep on the hill

News broke that infection had been found in a flock in Libanus, to the West of Cantref. Feelings were running high amongst local farmers who attended meetings in Brecon Barracks where DEFRA officials and Carwyn Jones, then the Welsh Minister of Agriculture (who eventually became First Minister in the Welsh Assembly Government), told them that foot-and-mouth had to be brought to a halt. The Beacons were to be a fire-break. All the hill sheep might have to be killed.

The farmers pleaded that these sheep from hefted flocks were the product of generations of clever, devoted shepherding. Hefted sheep know their particular geographic area (their cynefin). As with the farmers who own them, knowledge of the hills is passed on from generation to generation. The deep-seated fear was that if these hefted flocks were lost, hill farming in the Beacons and other upland areas of Britain, would never be the same again.

But the decision had been made and the slaughtering began. By mid-August twenty thousand or more sheep had been culled, creating a three-kilometre-wide fire-break. Conspiracy theories abounded. There were suspicions that the EEC and the British Government were so keen to stop paying subsidies to hill farmers that they were happy to take advantage of the opportunity to rid the uplands everywhere of sheep.

Every farmer has his or her own private experience of the cull. That it was profoundly distressing is not in doubt. Some went up to be with their animals. Some were angry. Some were stoical. Some cried. Some were physically sick. Some found it so unbearable they just had to leave the farm while it went on.

Tony Birdwood, a field officer working for the Rural Inspectorate for Wales with Operation Beacon said, "I remember especially watching a farmer in his late 60s just collapsing in tears on the hill when we told him that his flock had to go. Many people are so used to seeing the detached nature of people who farm massive areas and great numbers of cattle and sheep – they forget the absolute involvement of the Welsh hill farmer: his stock means almost as much to him as his family."

The local Health Trust set up phone lines to give counselling. One farmer said: "I feel guilty. I have let down the flock. I have let down my parents and grandparents and all those who built all this up."

Farmers have to keep a log of what happens to each sheep they own. This is one terse entry:

"12th August 2001: Lost all our hill flock owing to foot-and-mouth rules. They were gathered, blood-tested and shot. The blood results were clean. So they died for no reason."

As the blood tests came back, over and over again showing the animals were clean, the despair, depression and anger were palpable in the community. No-one knew what would happen next. Though the focus of attention had been on the farmers who had lost their stock, this was a situation with a massive ripple effect.

Farms neighbouring those affected could not buy or sell their stock either. And they still had to pay for feed and care for the animals. It has been argued that farmers whose stock was not culled but who nevertheless had to suffer enormous consequences, were as badly affected as those who lost stock.

On the Epynt, another quite different battle took place. The community came together in protest against the burning and burial of thousands of carcasses on land that was clean of any foot-and-mouth. The resulting battle was bitterly fought and won by the residents, but only after land had been contaminated. It was a catalogue of ineptitude, which left the community angry and scared.

Photograph Janet Foster

The local tourist industry was devastated. Walkers were banned from footpaths. Self-catering and bed-and-breakfast accommodation was empty; some went out of business. Liz Daniel, owner of Brecon Beacons Holiday Cottages, had to make several staff redundant. Millions of pounds were lost to the local economy.

Those who lost sheep were compensated. The rest of those who suffered did not get a penny. Here were the seeds of envy, discontent and division in the community. It would be naïve to say some of them did not take root. But the awfulness of what had happened seemed to eclipse even the most negative feelings. And slowly things began to regenerate.

And more than a decade later? Things were never going to be the same again and they are not. Some farmers decided enough was enough and retired or down-sized. The crisis highlighted the benefits of tourism to the local economy, and many farmers diversified into B & B and self-catering holiday accommodation. Cantref Adventure Farm grew from being a small trekking centre and caravan site to one of the Brecon Beacons' most popular attractions.

The hefted flocks have largely been re-established, helped by the fact that some sheep had been away on tack in unaffected areas, and returned to hills they knew after foot-and-mouth was over. Another nearby hefted flock was moved to a different part of the Beacons where it settled. A fence, put up to prevent the movement of stock during the fire-break exercise, has helped in the years following. Now there is huge controversy about whether it should be removed. Lovers of the open landscape versus farmers who value the ability to control the movement of stock vie with environmentalists who see potential in the situation for protection of species. The future of the fence remains one of the great unresolved issues.

But even the darkest times can be lit by bright moments. And, in the middle of it all, Liz and Terry Owen-Lowe were planning a big wedding for their daughter Sarah at Pontbren farm, where the flock had just been culled. Would the big day be cancelled? Would the majority of guests have to be stopped from coming? The answer was a resounding No!

Everyone turned out in their finery, and the huge celebration that followed lasted the entire weekend. The morning after, farmers in morning suits littering the field surrounding the marquee were a sight to behold!

Today the mood of the community is buoyant. Welsh lamb is a premium product and the tourist industry is thriving.

Was it all necessary? Would foot-and-mouth have been contained without the fire-break and the slaughter of thousands of healthy animals? The debate about vaccination, about the need for more local abattoirs, about the fairness of the compensation, about what should happen if, heaven forbid, it comes back – these are questions and issues which deserve a larger forum than this. This is the story of what happened in the fire-break - Where We Belong – Ein Cynefin.

This chapter was written with the help of research done by Christopher Russell-Jones who lived at Crofftau for 6 weeks during the foot-and-mouth epidemic and who interviewed many officials and farmers as part of a thesis for his degree at Oxford University in Human Geography.

Also of Jane Walters, Pannau, Cantref.

Marketing The Goods

In the end the goods must be sold. The chickens, eggs, herbs, butter, cheese, lamb, beef and pork, everything has to go to market and hopefully fetch a good price.

Market Day used to be a highlight of the week. This was a time for meeting friends and neighbours and exchanging news. While the women were shopping or selling their produce the men would be at the livestock market in the middle of Brecon. The noise and the smell and the population of the countryside would all come to Brecon on a Friday. The wonderful atmosphere of this big, gossipy, trading day in town will always been remembered and never recaptured. Today Brecon Livestock Market flourishes in its new venue, on the outskirts of town.

Emlyn Willaims loved taking cattle to Brecon Livestock Market – walking them all the way. Some stock was taken on a "gambo" or "float" pulled by horse.

As for fresh meat – this was killed in small local abattoirs or on the farm itself. A reminder of when meat came straight from the farm to the high street comes in a postcard, written in 1927, when Brecon butcher Mr. F. Maund put two halfpenny stamps on one of his own postcards, with a picture of his shop on the front.

The message on the back requested, "I could do with 6 lambs next Wed if suitable to you. Yours F Maund" The order was to Mr W Phillips of Pontbren farm and was no doubt completed to everyone's satisfaction. The postcard has survived as a testament to what many would consider a more gentlemanly, humane and efficient way of doing business.

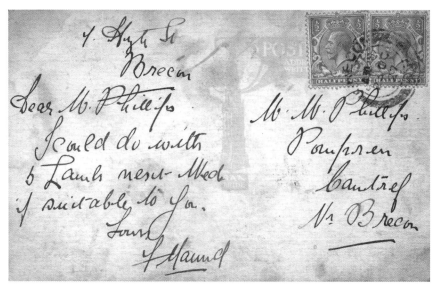

Mr. Maund's request to Mr. Bill Phillips

photograph courtesy of Brecknock Musum

Brecon Livestock Market 1905 – with gambos, floats and carts

The last Brecon Livestock Market in town – 1998

Artificial Rain in Wales!

In the 21st century marketing is not a social occasion. It's a science. Promoting Welsh Lamb has called for the best film directors and the finest copywriters. In 2007 a film crew from the award winning Ridley Scott Associates came to Crofftau,Cantref to see what it could do for Welsh Lamb.

Film crew under the umbrella with sprinklers and hose pipes making rain

The storyline began "We don't mind a spot of rain in Wales – its good for the land and good for the lamb". It required a lot of rain on a Welsh mountain. Not a problem you might think. But just in case there was no rain on the days they were filming the production team ordered up a fire engine and several bowsers of water.

And they were right because although it was pretty misty, it didn't rain. So the rain in the Welsh lamb advert is actually water pouring from an enormous sprinkler above Crofftau. It was a very funny sight. The advert, narrated by actor Mathew Rhys, was a hit. It improved the sales of Welsh Lamb by 40%.

From Hippy to Holiday Queen

It's not only food production that is responsible for a healthy economy in the Brecon Beacons today. Tourism has become a mainstay for a whole variety of local businesses. If one person could be credited with the booming market in self-catering accommodation in the Brecon Beacons, it is Elizabeth Daniel. Her relaxed but professional style has hit just the right note with owners and visitors alike.

Photograph Paul Campbell

Elizabeth Daniel, owner of Brecon Beacons Holiday Cottages

Elizabeth moved to Llanfrynach in 1972, and quickly made lifelong friends with her neighbours, artist Meg Stevens and an elderly aristocrat called Mrs Exham who was introduced to the village by her old friend Major Glyn de Winton.

"We were an unlikely trio," she says, "Me alone with two children, Mrs Exham a widow who could barely boil an egg, and Meg, who would be found on her artists stool, painting in fields and hills all over the Beacons, and who was wonderful, my rock for many years.

"The Rector, Revd Peter Sims, was a really keen fisherman – but not one of the most organised of people. He offered to teach my friend and me to fish, and loaned us some waders. She and I walked into the river after him and started to cast. Suddenly we both realised we could hardly move. The waders were full of holes and had filled with water up to our thighs! I'm not sure how we got out."

Llanfrynach proved an ideal home for Liz, who freely admits to being thought of as "Something of a scatty hippy – though I don't think I was really". But it was when farmer Donald Jones, Pentwyn, asked her to fix up an empty cottage and see if it could be let, that her future career was launched. Liz became one of Wales' most successful businesswomen; she has been at the forefront of helping farmers diversify by letting holiday cottages, and has done an enormous amount to promote tourism in the Beacons.

Originally a country girl from Surrey, Liz says she always imagined being a farmer's wife. Becoming the creator and owner of Brecon Beacons Holiday Cottages was not something she says, "I had pictured in my wildest dreams. I had no business aspirations at all." Besides having no business ambition, Liz also confesses to a limited ability with maths. But she says she has a "Good nose for people", and she surrounds herself with staff who understand bookkeeping and all the other things essential to ensure the smooth marketing and booking of 350 self-catering cottages in the Brecon Beacons.

Tourism is booming in the Beacons. Liz thinks there are several reasons, the most important being accessibility. "Chuck a bag in the boot, and in no time you can be in the heart of countryside which feels a million miles away from the city. Brecon Beacons National Park is still the least visited National Park in the country and the least commercialised, both of which increase its attraction for many people. And these days the food is good, very good."

Tourism was badly hit by the outbreak of foot-and-mouth disease in 2001. In one week alone Liz says that she cancelled 242 bookings, a loss of £74,000 to owners of the cottages. On top of that all the money the visitors would have spent in the community was lost. Liz had to lay off staff and was frightened for the future of her business.

The solution was bitter-sweet: Liz had just enough money to keep going by virtue of a small inheritance following the death of her parents. Within a few years the market had bounced back, with many farmers, realising that they needed an extra source of income, converting buildings for self-catering and now enjoying welcoming visitors to the area.

But for Liz, the Beacons are her home: she puts community first and business second. "I really don't like many people letting cottages in the middle of villages," she says, "it takes too much out of the community. If there are buildings on farms that can be used as holiday cottages while the farming continues, and maybe one day become a home for older parents or younger family members, then that is great."

Where Are We Going?

Pony trekkers from Cantref Adventure Farm head towards the Beacons

The foot-and-mouth crisis certainly meant a change of direction for Cantref Riding Centre, owned by Mary Evans, her son Colin and his wife Gwen, when they had to close for nearly 12 months.

It was time to think about what to do next, and they decided to concentrate on developing the kind of place where the whole family could enjoy a day out together. By 2004, Colin and Gwen had completely revamped the old Riding Centre and opened the new Adventure Farm. The following year, 2005, Cantref Adventure Farm won the UK Farm Attraction of the Year Award.

The horses at Cantref come in all shapes and sizes - to cater for all shapes and sizes of customers. Finding ponies with just the right temperament is very important, so Colin and Mary have started to breed some of their own horses on the farm.

Upper Cantref is still a working sheep-farm, but today the sheep are kept company by a whole variety of animals, including water-buffalo, llamas, alpacas, Shetland ponies, rheas and many small pet animals.

The development of the indoor play area and café has meant that in 2010 Cantref Harvest Supper could return to Upper Cantref and continue to host the Community Christmas Party folowing the carol service in nearby Cantref Church.

Community Spirit – What People Want

Out-of-town supermarkets, and the shutting of shops, Post Offices and schools have had a dramatic impact on community life in villages all over Britain.

Today, many village and country residents commute to Brecon, Merthyr and Cardiff to earn a living. The days when you could bank on bumping into your neighbours going about their daily business are long gone. Keeping community spirit alive takes real commitment and enthusiasm.

Llanfrynach Community Council, in conjunction with Brecon Beacons National Park Authority, conducted an in-depth survey to find out what people want from where they live in the future. It was no surprise to discover that what they still value, almost more than anything else, is a healthy and vibrant community.

The Community Council Consults Residents
Rita Williams, Cllr Gaynor Skyrme, Cllr Howard Vaughan, Cllr Val Jones and Gordon Jones

A few years ago, after much controversy, new houses were built on the edge of Llanfrynach. New residents have undoubtedly brought fresh energy and commitment into the business of community life. The consultation exercise helped to ignite an already smouldering spark of enthusiasm, with a number of very positive results.

Llanfrynach and Cantref Community Hall is being given a makeover, the children's playground has got new equipment, and Llanfrynach Summer Fête and Sports, together with other community events, provide the chance for everyone to relax and make friends. The Community Council brings out a regular newsletter to keep everyone informed about local events.

Photograph Jan Euden

Just some of the Tŷ Bach – Llanfrynach – Loo gang:
Steve Williams, Tony Bracey, Sue Brook, Jackie Williams, Rhidian Jones

Which brings us to the present day and the story of Tŷ Bach – Llanfrynach – Loos. In 2008, Powys County Council said the public conveniences in the village were too expensive to run and closed them down. Volunteers, led by Rhidian Jones, Tony Bracey and Steve Williams, decided to do the job themselves. The loos were scrubbed and painted, pictures and hanging baskets were put up – along with a collecting box. A rota of volunteer cleaners was organized. Llanfrynach Community Council gave the project its backing.

Today a visit to the Tŷ Bach provides locals and tourists alike with a clean, nicely decorated community-run loo. Not quite the sybaritic experience that was offered by the Roman Bath House – but very convenient all the same.

People have been very generous when spending a penny, which has enabled the Tŷ Bach to be twinned with toilets in the Giharo Commune of Rutana Province, Burundi – a small way of helping to address the fact that bad sanitation is one of the world's biggest killers, and every minute three children under five die because of dirty water and poor sanitation.

Hill Farming Today

Hill farming and hill farmers have changed. Once this was a life lived on the edge. Fear of crop failure, of losing stock to bad weather or disease, cast a long shadow over relentlessly hardworking lives. For many smallholders and labourers, subsistence living and survival was all they could hope for. Today, most hill farmers choose not to have all their eggs in one basket.

The current generation is not moving out, but it is moving on. Men and women, cut from hill farming cloth, have used their experience to widen their horizons, and have started a variety of new businesses: fencing, large agricultural machinery contracting, production of specialist food, self-catering holidays. All these and more are creating jobs and ensuring a healthier base for the local economy.

Inheritance has been a problem that has long troubled farmers. Which son should get the land? Traditionally women never got a look in as long as there was a son around. And, if there is more than one son, will splitting the farm mean it is no longer viable?

The increase in the divorce-rate also creates problems. Should the departing partner get half the value of the farm – and jeopardise the whole business? Divorce is probably no more common in the farming community than anywhere else, but it does pose a very particular set of extra and difficult dilemmas.

And today a new kind of person has entered the farming business scene – the tourist. Barns and cowsheds, no longer suitable for modern animal husbandry, make ideal conversions for people wanting a country holiday. The huge variety of people who find a week spent walking, trekking, white-water rafting, bird-watching or just lazing about is enriching the local mix.

But the main business of the Beacons is still the production of food. Since World War II, subsidies have ensured better security for the farmer and cheaper food for the consumer. Some say this is at the expense of the countryside with habitats being destroyed, overgrazing spoiling the hills, and the consumer having an unrealistic view of the actual cost of the food on their plate.

Farming in the 21st Century
Baling hay in the Beacons – Andrew "Flash" Phillips, Tylebrythos, Cantref

Hill farmers rely heavily on subsidies, but now instead of being paid per head of stock, the farmer is paid a subsidy per hectare. The intention is to create a better balance between how much lamb or beef the market will buy at realistic prices, and the desire to conserve the precious environment for the future. Schemes like Tir Gofal and Glastir have proved controversial, but look like being the way forward.

Each farmer has his own story to tell, and to describe one as 'typical' is never going to be accurate. But Thomas Jones Pentwyn is not 'untypical' of his generation. He comes from a long line of hill farmers on both sides of his family – the Jones's and the Richards's.

Though he has spent time away, in the end he returned to the hill farmed by his father, Donald Jones. His partner Hannah Starkey is a local solicitor and their three children, Finn, Rowan and Nia are all at the local school.

Chwarae Teg (Fair Play)
Thomas Jones, Pentwyn, Cantref – In charge of the sack-race

Thomas is as likely to be seen at the school gate as out on a tractor. The family all enjoy the visitors to their campsite and self-catering holiday accommodation. Like many locals, Thomas loves the feedback they get from visitors who are thrilled to find something different and special when they discover the Beacons, and he is happy to give them a glimpse of the lambing shed and his new pigs.

For this family, it is a lifestyle that works, with plenty of variety: farming, community, country, visitors and regularly going away to visit family and friends elsewhere.

Whilst it is easy to romanticise the 'good old days' of farming in the Beacons, the present has a lot to be said for it. And the future is full, not only of challenges to be faced, but of possibility.

How Do You Keep Her Down on the Farm?

The change in the role of the farmer's wife in the last century has probably been one of the biggest of all. As a young woman, Joyce Bufton wanted to qualify in food hygiene and nutrition – so in order to get work experience she took a job at Tregaer Farm. She was 19 and she fell in love – not only with farming life but also with the farmer, Gwynne Griffiths.

Joyce did go on to obtain a diploma in nutrition and physiology but she never left Tregaer. She and Gwynne had three children: John, Sally and Richard, and she took on the traditional role of farmer's wife. Asked why she had chosen to stay on the farm rather than go for a career she says: "It was a really interesting life. It had everything in it and I have never regretted it for a moment."

Like every other farmer's wife of her generation, Joyce would regularly cook for all the workers – ten to fifteen a night for supper was not unusual, especially on threshing or shearing days. Cows were milked by hand and at Tregaer, she churned 16 lbs of butter a week to sell in the market for Gwynne's uncle and aunt.

Today she considers the life of the farmer as potentially a lonely one, a solitary man out in a field on his modern tractor. One of the things she loved about farm life in her youth was that is was a very social one. The fact that farming used to be so labour-intensive meant lots of people, constantly coming and going.

Joyce remembers the children having a day off school to help in jobs like harvesting. Today, the combine harvester makes short and efficient work of the task. Farmer's wives leave home every day and have careers of their own and Joyce worries that increased self-reliance can mean loneliness for the farmer.

A full-time farmer's wife today would not be expected to thrive on the pickings to be gained from selling butter or eggs at the market as her only source of housekeeping money. And it is hard today to imagine the daily round of the exhausting tasks involved in cooking and cleaning without even running water on hand – a relentless routine punctuated by frequent childbirth.

Maybe it is only with the hindsight of modern comforts and freedoms that the negative side of the lives of many women of earlier generations can be viewed more clearly.

Whilst some women still choose to stay at home, looking after children and happily joining in the day-to-day running and management of the farm, many have developed parallel careers; nursing, the law, teaching, management, catering: women today make a different kind of contribution, but still manage to put in masses of hard work on the farm.

In an article in the local newsletter, Michelle Davies Pencaefadog described how each year she takes her annual spring holiday from work as a dental nurse to spend two weeks in the lambing shed. "If I'm lucky I'll get out to the swede field or escape to town for supplies for the sheep and us. It makes me cross when people say I'm not a proper farmer's wife because I work full-time away from the farm, but I think, like hundreds of others, I do my bit, after all this is what women do best, multi-tasking, only this is on a large scale. Some holiday eh!"

One thing that is still as popular as ever is a great country wedding with the happy couple leaving church to the sounds of the bells ringing, an archway of pikels held by Young Farmers and a huge party to follow.

There were two in Cantref in 2010 – the brides are both active farmers' wives but both have careers: Tracey Evans is a chemical process operator and Kate Phillips is training to be an accountant.

Tracey says, "It's quite difficult to explain what I do, most people get bored before I finish. Some people locally believe I have a top-secret job in the chemical industry, because I usually avoid questions about it! Not even Aub (her husband) understands what I do. I'm lucky enough to work shifts so have quite a lot of time off, this helps during lambing, harvest and other busy times.

"I would say that although I love my job and couldn't imagine not having my own money and independence, I also love working on the farm and miss it when I'm away at work. The reality of most farmers' wives working is it's a necessity rather than a choice; the average hill farm doesn't make enough money to support a family solely on that income.

The New Crop of Farmer's Wives

Mr and Mrs (Aubrey and Tracey) Evans
21st August 2010

Mr and Mrs (Mark and Kate) Phillips
11th September 2010

Centuries of Religious Life

The Brecon Beacons are littered with evidence of worship going back into the mists of time. Standing stones, circular sites, Bronze-Age cairns and stone circles are all evidence of belief and ritual that predate Christianity by thousands of years.

The combination of a cross on a circle that makes up the Celtic cross, is a reminder that nearly two thousand years ago early Christians made their mark on a people to whom the circle was sacred.

Photograph Ivor Jay

Celtic Cross in the Churchyard of St Cynidr and St Mary, Cantref

By the 4th century Christianity, was the official religion of the Roman Empire. So the Romans who lived in the villa and lounged in the wonderful baths in Llanfrynach (see p4) would probably have been at least nominally Christian. But it is not thought they went about converting the locals away from whatever religion they had at the time.

It wasn't until the Romans had left in the late 4th century that the first of the 'Celtic Christians' arrived in this part of Wales. They were not an organised Church but individuals, each trying to live what they interpreted as a Christian life.

The Beacons Benefice and its Celtic Saints

Susan Brook and Robert Soldat

Llanhamlach Church is dedicated to St. Peter and St. Illtyd (c. 450 – 527/537). Illtyd was one of the first Celtic Christians. He was born in Brittany, and legend has it that he crossed the Channel to join his relative King Arthur as a knight. A romantic bit of historical gossip says that Illtyd was one of three knights entrusted by Arthur with the Holy Grail, (the other two were St. Cadoc and St. Peridor), and even that Illtyd was actually Sir Galahad. Disappointingly both these legends are of dubious veracity at best.

Tŷ Illtyd, Llanhamlach

The story relates that Illtyd later left King Arthur and went on to serve the King of Morgannwg (Glamorgan). It was while he was there that he converted to Christianity and became a monk.

He started his new life as an ascetic hermit, but before long had attracted a number of followers, and the monastic community of Llan Illtyd was formed. The name was later contracted to Llantwit – known today as Llantwit Major. As well as being a teacher and leader, Illtyd had a practical bent, and one of his achievements is said to have been an improved design for a plough. The most famous of Illtyd's pupils was Dewi, (or David), who became St. David, Dewi Sant, the patron Saint of Wales.

More than half a dozen churches in the Brecon Beacons are dedicated to St. Illtyd, indicating that he had a serious following in the area. Above Libanus are Mynydd Illtyd and the almost circular churchyard of Llanilltyd. Nearby is Bedd Gwyl Illtyd, a Bronze-Age round barrow, allegedly his burial place.

Another site associated with him is Tŷ Illtyd, (Illtyd's House), in a field (on private land) in Llanhamlach; a chambered dolmen or quoit, presumably a tomb of Neolithic date, which Illtyd is said to have used as a place of retreat. Inside the tomb are drawings including a Roman lyre, a now illegible inscription and many small Christian crosses – a very unusual feature in a pre-Christian tomb.

From Tŷ Illtyd you look down towards the semi-circular site of Llanhamlach Church, which contains an important pre-Norman memorial stone, the Moridic stone, with the stylised figures of a man and woman on the front and a Latin inscription on the side. Who the figures are is uncertain – possibly Adam and Eve, or St. John and the Virgin Mary, or the female figure may be an obscure local saint, St. Eilewedd.

Today the Church is beautifully kept with new lighting, the stone walls round the church yard repaired and a new two-manual Ahlborn organ that means that Christine Morgan can continue to develop the already strong music tradition there.

One of the Beacons favourite and most respected artists, Robert MacDonald, has beautifully recreated old wall paintings of angels, which were crumbling.

Photograph David Morgan

Detail of the Restored Angels, painted by Robert MacDonald

168

Though the life of St. Illtyd has been the subject of much fascinating speculation – not much of it well-founded - even less is known about the other two saints of the Beacons Benefice, St. Brynach and St. Cynidr.

Llanfrynach Church is dedicated to St. Brynach (c. 570 AD). He was brought over from Ireland by Brychan, King and founder of Brycheiniog, to be his soul friend (Welsh: periglor), in other words Brynach's confessor, chaplain and spiritual adviser. It seems probable that his Llan (Church) was where the present church of Llanfrynach, holy place of Brynach, is today.

Photograph Janet Foster

St. Brynach's Church, Llanfrynach

The oldest part of the church is the tower, dated to the late 12th/early 13th century, substantially built with unusually thick walls, most probably for defensive purposes. The nave and chancel fell into a dilapidated state by the early part of the 19th century and was demolished in 1855/56 to be rebuilt by the Brecon architect and builder, William Jones.

A pillar stone in the church, believed to date from the 10th or 11th century, is carved with crosses, interlaced patterning and a figure with his hands raised, either preaching or in the posture believed to have been used by the early Celtic Christians for ecstatic prayer.

Llanfrynach Church has the largest churchyard in Breconshire or Radnorshire. In 2010, the Community Payback Scheme organised by the Welsh Probation Trust, undertook a major reclamation job to clear brambles and weeds, and a local appeal paid for new gates at the end of the yew walk.

Not much is known about St. Cynidr (c. 600 AD), to whom Cantref Church was originally dedicated. His mother Kehingayr (Ceingair) was a daughter of Brychan.

Cynidr lived principally in Breconshire with connections to the neighbouring borderlands of Radnorshire and Herefordshire. His most important base was at Y Clas-ar-Wy, otherwise Glasbury, where he is buried.

Photograph Garfield Kennedy

The Good Shepherd and Hill Lamb
Detail from altar window, St Cynidr and St Mary's Church, Cantref

Cantref Church has a quiet stillness in its churchyard, immaculately kept by neighbour Peter Jenkins. Inside there is some lovely stained glass – the altar window, appropriately for its hill farming community, features the Good Shepherd holding a hill lamb – you can tell by its whiteness and the smallness of its ears. All the biblical references to shepherds, flocks and lost-and-found sheep have a real resonance here.

Christmas, Easter, Harvest, hatching, matching and dispatching – there is no shortage of services, ceremonies and rituals to fill the churches. But as with many other congregations in small rural communities, attracting regular worshippers is a constant challenge. The three congregations had traditionally waited their turn for a Sunday service, with committed but dwindling attendance at each one.

What everyone enjoyed were the months when there were five Sundays, which always meant a joint service – more people, more fellowship and better singing! Why wait for a fifth Sunday? This was the question answered by a decision that all our services should be joint, and all three congregations would go to each others' services.

The Archdeacon of Brecon, Ven Randolph Thomas
with Revd David Thomas, born and bred in Cantref.
Waiting for the bride to arrive at Cantref Church

The result was that when the new Priest-in-Charge, the Archdeacon of Brecon, Ven Randolph Thomas, arrived in September 2006, a much healthier Church community had begun to grow. Under his leadership this mutual support and co-operation has ensured a much healthier congregation each week, and the continued existence of a church in each community.

But perhaps even more importantly, the congregations are mutually supportive and work hard to maintain, not only the fabric, but also the worship and Christian spirit of the Benefice.

One of the great features of the Benefice is that the peak of Pen y Fan is in one of its parishes – Cantref. In July 2007, hundreds of people trekked to the summit on an occasion that was called 'Walk to Worship', with a service at the top jointly conducted by the then Bishop, Rt Revd Anthony Pierce, and the Archdeacon.

It proved a challenging climb for some! But the triumph of reaching the top of the mountain and singing 'Bread of Heaven' and 'Calon Lân' very loudly, made all the effort worthwhile!

Walk to Worship July 2007

Photographs Daniel Leyland

More than 300 people walked to the service at the top of Pen y Fan

One member of the crowd on top of Pen y Fan that day was Jonathan Morgan. His face is a familiar one in all parts of Breconshire life. He gives his tireless support to many charities, particularly L'Arche and Combat Stress; he works energetically in politics, locally and internationally, and loves music, singing, conversation and his many friends.

His story, told next, of coming home from service with the armed forces, must be the untold story of many soldiers returning from duty, shattered by their experiences. Jonathan believes that the support and solace he found in his community were vital to his recovery.

Reflections on coming Home
To Breconshire and Llanfrynach

Jonathan Morgan

On Top
Jonathan – at the summit of Pen y Fan

Having spent ten years in the armed forces, most of it in the Royal Regiment of Wales, I was most relieved to be able to come back to my parents' lovely cottage in Llanfrynach.

It had been a long journey, which started as a young boy watching the parades of South Wales Borderers marching through their home town of Brecon. It was often with a lump in the throat and great pride that we watched.

The countryside around Brecon was littered with the sometimes-grand houses of former officers of the Borderers, including the de Wintons and Lloyds in Llanfrynach. I was star-struck by the glamour of it all.

Army service took me to the desert and the jungle and gave me a four-month tour of duty in the Ardoyne in Belfast in 1972 that was hell.

Finally I cracked: I discovered that I hated violence, hated being out of my beloved Wales and disliked taking orders.

173

I returned to Llanfrynach a broken man. I had to go into hospital at Talgarth, and it was then that three things started working on my psyche: firstly the beauty of nature in the Beacons and the Black Mountains, secondly the feeling of community and being welcomed back without reservation, and thirdly the beautiful music all around, in the churches especially.

Religion, exercise and music were to nurse me back to health, together with the friends I had nurtured and who had nurtured me, many of them around Llanfrynach, including my second home Llanbrynean, where the Harpurs provided me with huge warmth and hospitality.

The White Swan pub was like a second university, with the Rector, Peter Sims, holding court. Mental health is always said to be helped by space and access to the countryside; I had plenty of this in Llanfrynach, and perhaps of all things trees were significant; we have so many magnificent ones around here.

Slowly the healing of nature took hold, helped by the slower pace of the countryside and the succession of the seasons. My time of recuperation was punctuated by long walks in the Beacons and getting to know the village cricket team with all the fun that entailed.

It was not quite a return to those Edwardian bucolic days experienced by the likes of Sassoon and Graves of my own regiment, but it was not far off that feeling. I had some idea of how my father felt returning after five years as a prisoner of war. To belong to a community is so important to the returning war veterans, and I was so lucky I had Llanfrynach.

In 2010 Jonathan Morgan published his book Rags to Riches: Entrepreneurs of Welsh Origin

The Reverend Peter Sims

Revd Peter Sims and his wife Cathy and family lived in the Rectory at Llanfrynach for 23 years. As Rector, he had the living of Llanfrynach, which meant, unlike most priests today, he did not have to move parishes every few years. He was also Rector of the churches in Cantref and Llanhamlach.

Revd Sims' ability to connect with children was evident in the lively Sunday school he ran and the nativity plays and fancy dress parades he organised for the young people. Stephanie and Brian Williams, who farmed at Cefn Cantref, say his encouragement of their three sons gave them, and other young people, self-confidence and a great start in life. He had a magnificent singing voice. In Cantref Church, when there was often no-one to play the organ, he would announce the hymn with the words, "I will sing the first two lines then you can all join in". And the singing, unaccompanied, was wonderful.

Back: Mrs Merrick, Revd Sims, PC Nigel George
In Front: Eleanor Sims, Stephanie Hopkins, Fiona Austin, Carol Eckley, Tom Bowcher

Revd Peter Sims at Llanfrynach School's
Cycling Proficiency Certificate Presentation 1980s

Jonathan Morgan remembers conversations with him in the White Swan as like being at a "mini university". His interests were the arts, literature, especially Shakespeare and fishing. Stories about Peter are legion. Elizabeth Daniel has a one about him trying to teach her to fish *(page 155)*. Peter Sims had that otherworldly quality which is the hallmark of many an academic. His intelligence, amiability and conviviality are fondly remembered.

The Best Job in the World

Jon Pimm – Warden with Brecon Beacons National Park Authority

It could be billed as 'The best job in the world' – where else could you repair a footpath in the shadow of Pen y Fan, help a stranded motorist, negotiate with an illegal off-roader and lead a nature walk all in one day?

Jon Pimm fixing a signpost to the Beacons

I've been a National Park Warden for almost 10 years. I started at the grassroots, so to speak, when I worked as an Assistant Area Warden and then I was promoted to Area Warden in 2004.

National Park Wardens undertake a wide variety of jobs. We liaise with landowners, lead guided walks, clear paths and repair fragile landscapes, and also work with educational groups and the National Park Visitor Centres. In the last few years we have worked closely with the police, mountain rescue teams and other emergency services to keep residents and visitors safe when they are in the National Park.

The National Park covers an area of 520 sq miles stretching from Pontypool in the South all the way to Hay-on-Wye in the North, and from the edge of Abergavenny in the East to the edge of Llandeilo in the West.

The wardens divide Brecon Beacons National Park up into two areas, East and West. I work for the Western Area Team and, luckily for me, the dividing line runs right along the side of the community of Llanfrynach in the West, where I now live.

I'm a relative newcomer to Llanfrynach – I've only lived here for two years – but part of its attraction was the imposing sight of Pen y Fan (886 metres above sea level), which overshadows, yet somehow shelters, our small village. As well as living in Llanfrynach I work with the communities and landowners all the way from Brecon, through to Libanus and the Central Beacons, and then all the way to Manor Mawr, near Penderyn.

I also look after sites owned by the National Park Authority such as Cantref Wood – a small woodland outside Llanfrynach - home to a sea of bluebells in May and one of my favourite places in the Park. This special place is evidence that you can still find places of natural beauty, which also offer extreme solitude.

Photograph Brecon Beacons National Park

Volunteers repairing a Dry Stone Wall on the Beacons

A crucial role for me is maintaining the rights of way in my area. One of the most controversial issues we face is illegal off-roading, particularly on the Gap Road that runs through the community of Cantref. In November 2006, as part of the Natural Environment and Rural Communities Bill, roads used as public paths, like the Gap Road, were reclassified as Restricted Byways. This change was very important because it removed the vehicular rights to use the road, effectively making it an offence to drive a mechanically propelled vehicle on the Gap Road.

The Gap Road had been a very popular place for off-roading and many drivers and motorbike riders continue to use it even now. We are working hard with Powys County Council to try and make it absolutely clear that the legislation means that it is illegal to take any mechanical vehicle there.

177

In April 1996, Brecon Beacons National Park Authority (BBNPA) came into being, when it replaced the former Brecon Beacons National Park Committee, which had managed the Park since 1974.

National Parks have two statutory purposes: - to conserve and enhance the natural beauty, wildlife and cultural heritage, and to promote opportunities for public enjoyment and understanding of its special qualities. National Park Authorities must also foster the economic and social well-being of communities living within them as well as nurturing a sense of pride.

But it's not just the staff of the Brecon Beacons National Park that make up the workforce. We rely heavily on a dedicated volunteer force, people who give their time freely on a variety of projects. They work in all weathers leading guided walks, building stiles and repairing footpaths, staffing car-parks and disseminating information to residents and visitors. The National Park is grateful for their unwavering support because without them our jobs would be made an awful lot harder.

One of the major challenges for BBNPA today is to balance the conservation of this beautiful and fragile environment with the needs of the thriving local communities. Providing opportunities for sustainable innovative development – particularly with the onset of climate change – is one of the biggest tests we face. But for people in this remote area of the Brecon Beacons there is hope for a more sustainable future, largely thanks to our communities uniting to tackle these challenges head on.

Innovative concepts are being introduced on sustainable design, hydroelectric installations and other renewable energy and carbon-cutting initiatives. Small ideas like litter picking schemes and community owned allotments and orchards have bloomed into bigger ideas including producing timber from community-managed woodland schemes, installing solar energy panels, buying electric cars and bikes which the whole community can use, restoring peat bogs in order to hold onto carbon, car sharing, reinstating old water mills and bio-diesel clubs.

For me, living and working in this beautiful place, these projects give me hope that there will still be a National Park when I am too old to get up the hills to see it from the tops.

Waterfalls and Rivers

Photograph Phil Taylor

Waterfalls in the Cwm Sere. with Cribyn behind

Countless rills and mountain streams plunge down the Brecon Beacons to join the Usk, the Wye, the Taf and the Nedd. Magnificent waterfalls abound on these mountain streams and rivers, enriching the beauty of the landscape. At their most powerful, they are a mighty force and at their most peaceful, an idyllic retreat. They are a fabulous habitat for fish and wildlife, and provide great pleasure to walkers, and exhilarating sports for the adventurous. Lower down in the main valleys, they provide wonderful opportunities for fishermen too.

The Good Samaritan

Leslie Williams

Alf Bevan was a full-time train driver who often worked on the Builth and Hereford routes. But when he was off duty, Alf was a keen fisherman. He often worked as a gillie at Abercynrig, Llanfrynach. One day he was on the Builth run, and could see a fisherman having difficulty landing a salmon he had hooked in the River Wye, which flowed parallel to the railway.

Alf Bevan – Train Driver and Fisherman

Like the Good Samaritan that he was, Alf stopped the train and hurried down to the river in order to help land the catch. Somehow the story was published in 'The Times' newspaper, which reported that Alf had a wonderful ovation from the passengers when he remounted his engine!

180

A Fishy Culture

Dr John Taylor

The Cynrig Fish Culture Unit, Llanfrynach, is situated on the River Cynrig, a tributary of the River Usk three quarters of a mile from the confluence of the two rivers. It was established in 1965 by the Central Electricity Generating Board to produce salmon smolts as compensation for losses in the River Usk caused by abstraction of water for cooling purposes by Uskmouth Power Station.

In 1986 the Unit was taken over By Welsh Water Authority and, following the privatisation of the water industry, by the National Rivers Authority in September 1989. In 1996, the National Rivers Authority ceased to exist, its duties being superseded by the newly-formed Environment Agency, which now owns and runs the Unit.

At present, Cynrig rears 100,000 salmon fry each year for the River Taf to mitigate the impact of the Cardiff Bay barrage on fish migration. Also 180,000 salmon fry are released annually into the River Wye to mitigate for lost spawning and nursery area caused by the construction of the Elan Valley reservoirs.

In addition to its work restoring fish stocks damaged by man's activities, Cynrig also runs several captive-breeding programmes for threatened or endangered aquatic species. These include the Freshwater Pearl Mussel (FWPM), the White-Clawed crayfish, the water vole and the Twaite shad.

The FWPM is functionally extinct in Wales but small pockets survive in certain areas. The young mussel is a parasite on the gills of juvenile salmonids, which play host to this species over the winter. In the spring the young mussels drop off the gills and burrow into the gravel; they can live up to 150 years of age. Unfortunately, habitat degradation, pollution and siltation have taken their toll, such that there are no young mussels evident in our rivers. However the breeding programme, coupled with habitat restoration, aims to release thousands of young mussels of 2 to 3 years of age to help establish a viable population.

Our native crayfish, the White-Claw, is being increasingly threatened by the presence of the non-native American Red-Claw (brought in for farming in the 1970's), which carries a fungal plague. The Red-Claw crayfish is resistant to the plague, whereas any contact is lethal for the White-Claw. Juvenile crayfish have been successfully bred at Cynrig for research and re-introduction into plague-free 'ark sites'.

The Water Vole (Ratty from Wind in the Willows) is thought to be extinct in Powys due to loss of suitable habitat and predation by the introduced North American mink (introduced for the fur farming trade in the 1950's). However, suitable habitat has been created at the nearby Llangorse Lake, and an intensive mink-trapping programme has been undertaken in the last few years. Several hundred young voles have been reared at Cynrig hatchery and re-introduced into the newly created habitat and have successfully spread around the lake.

The numbers of Twaite shad (a bony Herring-like fish) entering our rivers from the sea have declined over the years to dangerously low levels. One theory is that the delicate young fry, on their migration route back out to sea, are being sucked into the myriad of pumped water intakes that now line our rivers. A commercial fisheries consultancy has been developing an acoustic scaring device to try and prevent the fish being drawn into these intakes. Cynrig has developed a breeding programme for shad in order to provide young fry for testing the efficacy of the acoustic deterrent.

Apart from these conservation breeding programmes, Cynrig also plays an important educational role running classroom salmon-egg incubator programmes and a water vole project with Llangorse School. The hatchery has over 500 visitors a year from schools, universities and local groups. Cynrig has also run several MSc and PhD student projects in conjunction with Swansea University.

Dr John Taylor 'stripping' a Wye salmon – watched by his daughters

Competition

No doubt country people do work hard – they shear sheep, bake cakes, train dogs, grow food. But they can have fun too. They just turn the day job into a competition, to see who is the best at sheep-shearing, cake-baking, marrow-growing, plough-furrowing, etc. etc.…. And for added spice they make up lots of rules. Winning is more about pride than prizes.

Most of these competitions happen at country shows. The biggest is the Royal Welsh Show in Llanelwedd, now the biggest agricultural show in Europe. Brecon Agricultural Show is the oldest and celebrated its 250th anniversary in 2005.

Practically every community can boast its own annual bash where prizes for all the above things and more, plus a variety of odd sports are all hotly contested. You can see it all through this book, – from wellie-throwing to leek-growing – country people love nothing more than a competition! And of course the most important of all is Rugby. Here are two champions!

Ernie Davies, Berllan

Throwing the Wellie Champion
Cantref Sports 2010

Tony Davies, The Wern
Grade III WRU referee and a touch judge
with the Welsh Premier League.
Ran the fastest time with his son Tom in a
wheelbarrow at Llanfrynach Sports 2010

Up the (Talyllyn) Junction!

Talyllyn Junction

Wales was a dry country on Sundays for centuries. But although the Welsh people actually voted to close all their pubs on the Lord's Day, they also managed to find various ingenious ways to ensure they could get round the rules.

On the East side of the Talyllyn Railway Tunnel (which ran through Greenway Farm, Llanhamlach, *(see page 57)* was the Talyllyn Junction. The refreshment room there, under the opening laws in Wales, was licensed to sell alcoholic refreshment to bona fide travellers, thus escaping the Sabbath prohibition that applied to pubs. So on Sundays, Bryan Williams of Greenway Farm and several others would 'travel' through the tunnel to the railway buffet for a perfectly legal beverage or two.

The refreshment room at Talyllyn was quite a local Mecca. Val Jones of Llanhamlach recalls: "When we were teenagers we used to get one of the older ones to go in and get us a drink. We didn't always get away with it – but when we did, we really enjoyed sitting outside and having the trendy tipple of the day - a Babycham. Gaynor Skyrme, Groesffordd, also has fond memories of Talyllyn but she preferred something called Bob-a-Nog. Sounds lethal!

Cheers!

Home brewing has always been a great local tradition. Apples and pears grow well on the lower ground down towards Llanfrynach. There were orchards at Berllan (which is ' Welsh for 'orchard'), at Abercynrig and at Upper Cantref. All this meant lots of cider and perry.

Fruit trees do not do so well high up in the Beacons, so in Cantref they brewed beer. On Saturdays in Cantref in the months after lambing and before harvest, the air was full of the smell of beer brewing. Each farm had a big pot in a shed where the beer was brewed to be drunk during heavy working days on the farm.

Quenching a thirst at the end of a hard days work harvesting.
The note on the back says, "A sample of our staff, David Rees"

Brewing the beer involved a lot of to-ing and fro-ing around the farms. The first step was to get the huge 50-gallon barrel, called a 'stun', in which the whole process was started off; this belonged to the Powells of Plas-y-Gaer. When the hops had been boiled, the mixture was put in the stun to cool down. On top of this went the balm, a live ingredient like yeast. This too was carried from farm to farm.

Teddy Trosnant says: "It was carried very carefully; if you bumped it about too much it would froth up and spill over and be lost". "Then," says his wife June, "there would be a big row!"

Because there was a better boiler at Pencaefadog, most of the brewing happened there. The beer was then decanted into 8-10 gallon barrels and delivered by a horse-drawn gambo (a cart usually used for hay at harvest) in another bumpy ride, over the fields to Trosnant.

Another favourite ingredient to add flavour to the beer was broom, which children were sent onto the hillsides to gather. Brewing was a job done in March and October, because there is less likelihood of a thunderstorm then, and thunder makes the beer turn sour. Drinking it, on the other hand, seemed to happen all year round.

According to Glenys Pugh it had a "Quiet, dead, flat sort of taste." The men didn't get drunk on it – they were working too hard. But the pub in Brecon on a Friday after market – well it seems that was a different matter!

Murray Rose, who used to live at Tyle Llwyd, said he found some stones, which appeared to be malting stones, in the undergrowth near the lane leading up to his home. One can imagine the local spirit made there might have staved off many a winter cold!

In Llanfrynach a mobile cider press was taken from farm to farm, including Upper Cantref, where they also had their own orchard. Abercynrig had its own cider press.

Sucking Cider Through a Straw

Leslie Williams

Until 1947, there were two cider apple orchards and one pear orchard at Abercynrig. One of the outstanding buildings at Abercynrig is the 'Wainscot', which houses a large permanent cider mill. A large solid stone wheel was mounted on an axle and pulled around the trough by a horse, which went around and around the mill until the stone wheel had crushed all the apples. The crushed apple, called "must" was then put on the press to extract the juice.

Pen and ink watercolour by Jenny Joice

Cider Mill at Abercynrig

Ron Harris on the left and Leslie Williams by the wheel

As boys, we didn't like the cider when it was corked down and stored; but during the fermenting period the apple juice was lovely and sweet, so we used to cut a long straw in order to drink the juice. It was never discovered, for there was always some of it in a can to top up the barrels. We made perry in exactly the same way. I am sure as boys we thought we were the only ones who had thought of this practice.

The older generation had a much stronger constitution than we have, for I remember that when the cider had really matured, our neighbour would already have been round his flock of sheep and would then call at the Mill when we were having breakfast. I always drew him a quart jug of cider, which he quaffed however cold the morning.

The Old Ford Inn, Llanhamlach

Liz Bramley, with recollections from
Elizabeth Elston, Jill Jones, Jenny Wilson-Jones and Robin Adams

This inn dates back to drovers' days and before, but my history of the Old Ford starts in 1950 when it was bought, as the New Inn, by Major Wilson-Jones MC. His three daughters, who were in their teens when they moved here from Buckinghamshire, remember how primitive the buildings were. There was a simple bar to the left of the front door, with one cold tap, and two rooms to the right, which were let out for meetings. The kitchen was a lean-to behind this, with a barn and outbuildings at the back. A chemical toilet provided sanitation across the yard, but men normally resorted to 'the great outdoors'.

The Anglo Brewing Company had owned the inn, and the daughters remember the previous innkeeper as an alcoholic ex-naval personality with firm views on what he would serve. When asked on one occasion for a particularly complicated round of drinks, he is reputed to have said: "What do you think I am, a *** chemist? Get out!"

Once settled in, the family built up the business by offering bed and breakfast, with dinner for residents. Amongst guests was Sir John Hunt of the 1953 Everest expedition, no doubt still drawn to exceptional mountain areas. Other clients came, often on foot, from Brecon, the surrounding villages and Merthyr; many were in the Army.

Major Wilson-Jones was a good raconteur, having spent five of his military years in the French Foreign Legion. He developed a friendly atmosphere where women felt comfortable. Often wives who came out with their husbands would pop into the kitchen and spend the evening with Mrs Wilson-Jones. Jenny described one all-female group, however, who said that they did not drink alcohol, but 'a little port and lemon would be fine'. After several of these, the ladies enjoyed a particularly merry evening.

The daughters give great credit to their mother, who had lived a relatively comfortable life and now found herself cooking for clients and managing a much larger domestic operation. One attraction at the Old Ford was undoubtedly the three younger Wilson-Jones 'barmaids', who often helped out for pocket money.

Apart from the convivial atmosphere indoors, they also created a pleasant garden behind the house. There was an orchard at the far end, where they also kept a variety of birds. Jill remembers the geese, particularly when one took off to the other side of the river and they ended up hunting for it in Pencelli.

Elizabeth summed up their situation: "We were very fortunate to come to such a lovely place." This is underlined by the fact that all three sisters still live close by.

The Old Ford Inn in the 1960s, with the Coronation Oak

When Major Wilson-Jones died suddenly in 1960, the Old Ford was sold to my parents, Dr and Mrs Adams. Together with my brother Robin, they developed the business, and four years later my parents moved into a new house built at the end of the orchard, where I now live with my husband, the business long-since sold.

My father, formerly a GP in Birmingham, took great delight in developing the restaurant trade, with good food and wine. He had served in India during the War and drew on his experience there to introduce the first curries in the area in 1961, when my brother's Indian friend Shivaji joined him as chef. Chicken in the basket was another firm favourite.

I recall the celebration when we first got into *The Good Food Guide*, which described the Old Ford as '...homely with comfortable touches like hot water bottles in the beds'.

The introduction of progressively stricter drink-driving legislation in the 1960s took some getting used to, and Robin often took regular clients home at the end of a Saturday evening.

In those days, a regular but infrequent bus service passed through Llanhamlach, and people from Pencelli would walk along the lane to the Old Ford Inn, crossing the River Usk at the ford below it with shoes tied round their necks, to get the bus to work in Abergavenny or Brecon. The 'ford' was already impassable to vehicles before this history, but the wide shingle banks at the lane (now shifted downstream), made it accessible for paddling across during most of the year.

The Coronation Oak, planted for Edward VII (c. 1901), had to be cut down in the early 1990s, and is only seen now in photographs.

Because it corresponds closely to my feelings, having returned to live 'Where I Belong' after a 40 years absence, I leave the last word to my father, writing in a medical publication in 1971 of his change in circumstances due to MS: '…our house is set into the side of a valley, and beyond the river there is a wide mountainous panorama. I always feel it is a better place than we would have normally retired to…'

The Hills Are Alive……

Musicians, artists, writers and film-makers looking for peace and quiet, spiced up by drama, discovered the Beacons years ago. Indeed some locals are pretty old hands at coping with the highs and lows of being an extra.

John Davies of Llanhamlach was 17 when Ealing Film Studios made a propaganda film about the guerrilla war that Marshal Tito was fighting against the Germans in Yugoslavia. Michael Wilding and Stanley Baker were the stars. John played both a German soldier and a partisan fighter, getting 'danger money' for dying in the river.

But by the time the film was completed, Tito had become a communist and sided with the Russians, so was no longer flavour of the month, and the film was mothballed. No starring role for John then! Eventually it was released with its name changed from 'Chetnics' to 'Under Cover'.

Tregaer Farm was the location for the Merchant Ivory film of H. E. Bates' 'Feast of July', which was set in the 1860's and which involved many local people as extras. Two fields of corn were especially sown, and local people were trained in the old skill of scything especially for the film.

In 1959, one of the great classics of British New Wave Cinema, Tiger Bay, brought to life the street culture of Cardiff's Bute Town. But although the film focused on the raw inner-city life, just a few of the scenes were filmed near Talybont-on-Usk. Libby Richards, whose family was famous for their Welsh Mountain Ponies, was put in charge of making sure they came into shot at just the right moment. The film starred John Mills and his daughter Hayley Mills in her first major film role.

Hayley Mills on a Welsh Mountain Pony
On location at Talybont–on–Usk for the film Tiger Bay, released in 1959

Meg Stevens

An evening with Meg Stevens, her paintings propped up round the Village Hall, she and all the women in the WI talking nineteen to the dozen – well, that was a great night out!

Llanfrynach and Cantref Women's Institute is enormously grateful to both Meg and her husband Roger for allowing her paintings to be used for the cover of the first 'Where We Belong', then for a WI Calendar to celebrate our 60th anniversary in 2009, and now two more paintings on the cover of this book.

In her painting prime Meg was a famous sight, out in all weathers, totally absorbed, capturing the natural life of the Brecon Beacons. Meg had obtained a Fine Arts degree (Reading University, 1954) and an MA (Leeds University, 1956). The latter specialised in Book Arts: illustration and wood engraving. She married Roger, who had been a fellow student, and in 1969/70 they moved, with their two daughters, Bridget and Hannah, to Llanfrynach when he began work with the Brecon Beacons National Park Authority.

It was about five years later that Meg really started in earnest to paint the world around her, in all seasons of the year – never in a studio!

In 1993, Meg produced a book about her work and herself. These words are taken from it and the second edition produced a few years later: "Usually paint within a few miles of home; where possible, riding ancient bike, with home-made easel carrier on the back. Sometimes use ageing Renault 5 as roadside shelter in winter – but even then have to have window open.

"If I find myself painting in places where I almost have to cling on with my teeth, it's because these are some of the only places left where wild flowers can grow in profusion, the way they are meant to. When I find a bit where they grow plentifully, I want to celebrate.

"All art makes a statement of some kind about something experienced, emotionally or physically. It may be in the nature of a protest, or a poem or a political statement. I think mine is a sort of celebration.

"One eventuality that I find hard to accept without protest, is that what you paint one week might have vanished by the next, sometimes for good. Ponds filled in, roadside flowers mown before seeding, hedges ripped out, municipal grass planted with alien shrubs and flowers, rather than native ones (which could support local wildlife) – or worse, kept mown bald, even of daisies.

"It's up to us – you and me – to fuss when such things happen. Ask questions. Put in a word for wildlife, which can't speak for itself. I do not have a studio. It's out there in the open. People are always telling me it's crazy. (It is. I guess one of these days somebody will pick me rigid out of a ditch!)

"Of course, all the best pictures reveal themselves when you haven't got your paints, are all dressed up going to somebody's wedding; or it is still light enough to see the view but too dark to see the colour of the paint.

Meg – in her studio!

"Every picture is a fight. It wouldn't be worth doing, I suppose, if it weren't. One suffers cold, heat, stiff neck, tennis-elbow. Brolly springs a leak, blows away. Easel collapses, seeds in one's socks and prickles in one's pullover.

"I can't decide if it's me fighting to find how to say it, or the picture fighting to get itself said. That they do somehow get themselves said, is not a tribute to my skill, but to the beauty which, in spite of all that we do to our environment, insists on breaking out wherever it finds the smallest chance."

Her devotion to painting here was single-minded for 25 years. In 1996 she was elected a Royal Cambrian Academician. She only faltered five years later, through a succession of stumbling blocks, including foot-and-mouth's restrictions on exploring the countryside, hip problems and – not surprisingly, reduced energy for hedgerows and ditches!

For Adele Nozedar, arriving at one of the most remote spots in an area that specialises in remote, it was love at first sight. She just knew it was the perfect place to make music. Torpantau, at the top of the Neuadd Reservoir, became her home and where she and Adam Fuest established The Twin Peaks Studio. Many of the country's top artists, including the Manic Street Preachers, Catatonia, Patrick Jones, David McAlmont, Mick Jones, Peter Doherty and Babyshambles, made and recorded music at Twin Peaks.

Echoes
Adele Nozedar

There's a very odd kind of one-upmanship that I've noticed that comes into play between people who are privileged to live in 'wild' landscapes. I suspect you'd have to live in one to know exactly what I mean; but, for example, I'll be the first to point out that my home is:

1. Nearly two thousand feet above sea-level (yes, imperial measurements may be old-fashioned, but using feet sounds higher than, and therefore superior to, the metric equivalent).
2. An hour and a quarter's walk to the nearest neighbours (who are incredibly nice).
3. A round trip of just over twenty-five kilometres if you run out of milk (you'll see how I've sneakily used metric measurements here for the same reason that I used imperial ones in point 1).

I live in the Brecon Beacons, on the south side of Pen y Fan. I moved here on 7th August 1994 after visiting Wales for the first time on 22nd July 1994. The full story is too bizarre and fantastical to go into here; it's enough to tell you that quitting the smelly, noisy, bad-tempered fug of London, which was never my home anyway, for the vast expanse of mountains, lakes, and the gentle kindliness of this precious part of Wales didn't take an awful lot of thinking about.

Subsequently, my ex-husband (who will always be my life-long friend) and I built an award-winning state-of-the-art recording studio on land that had never, ever been occupied or built on; the closest signs of habitation are the remains of a Bronze Age settlement some quarter of a mile away.

I often take visitors on the fifteen minute walk away from all the comforts of twenty-first technology, equipment and modems, flashing lights and air conditioning, through the lovely, squelchy, rotten-smelling mud to the place where the stone circles are, the entrances into these ancient homes still plainly marked by their threshold stones. The first time I found this place I was so excited I couldn't sleep.

Ancient stone circles in the ground by the Neaudd Reservoir

I love the way that people's minds are blown and their imaginations stimulated as time fizzles away, the sense of the space takes over, and a connection is made between us and the people who lived and died here some four thousand years ago.

Somehow this connection is unified by the simple act of treading on the same ground, the same rocks, and, who knows, maybe even squashing flat the same plants that these ancestors knew.

I will never take this place for granted, and I love seeing others' delight, too, in such simple things as jumping into the river on a hot summers' day, or seeing shooting stars in a night sky that's properly dark, or the experience, when the mountains are frozen white, of shouting into the nothingness and hearing that shout bounce between the peaks for up to five times.

All these pleasures are things that those ancient people would have enjoyed, too. Maybe they even took them for granted. I'd really love to see what they would make of our lives and all the things that I expect, despite the ancient landscape; electricity, hot and cold water coming out of taps, central heating. And the ability to record those echoes, too, if I wanted.

Tales – Tall and Not So Tall

When the embers are glowing in the fire and a glass of something has been taken, is the time to reminisce and to tell a few tales – tall and not so tall. Here are a few.

One of the oldest stories of all must be about the ghostly apparitions in a field near the Roman remains in Llanfrynach. In 1698, Thomas ap John's grandson Hugh Thomas wrote a detailed history of Brecknockshire in which he describes the Roman Baths at Maesderwen and the two fields Cairney Bach and Clos y Gevelin being covered in Roman cinders.

In a corner of a field called Cae Croff, Thomas said a great treasure of money was hidden. He related that many people had attempted to dig a pit there to discover the hoard; but instead of finding treasure, they had been frightened away by apparitions. A similar story was also told about the cairn at Manest Court, Llanhamlach. But maybe there is a more rational explanation behind these scary tales.

Wraiths, Roman Cinders and a Chemist
Dave Hope

Did you know that no less a person than Henry Vaughan visited Llanfrynach in the 1600s and recorded his experience in his book 'Towards a 16th Century History of Brecknock'. On his visit he met some villagers who described how they had gone digging in a field near the village – the field of cinders - looking for treasure. As they dug, wraiths appeared and some men became blind, some lame and some mad. He actually met these men – so the story was probably genuine … wasn't it?

Well that would have been the end of things had I not met an actual ghost-hunter at a Christmas dinner party. He was a retired chemist who had worked at Llanwern steelworks. He explained that over 98 per cent of supposed hauntings could easily be explained by science and few were really inexplicable.

Over a pint at the bar I told him of the Henry Vaughan reference and suggested he might visit Llanfrynach to see if there were any spooky remnants floating about. Taking a moment of thought and a pull of his glass, he asked if there was a Roman villa site nearby – which of course there is in Llanfrynach. He then offered the following explanation of the haunting.

The Roman villas, as every school child knows, had hypocausts beneath them – the original under-floor heating. For fuel the Romans probably brought coal on packhorses from the coal patches near the Heads of the Valleys road. Along the Roman Road of course.

Now the hypocausts were probably very inefficient at burning the coal and when they cleared out the grate, as it were, there could have been plenty of unburned coal amongst the cinders. The cinders were then dumped outside the villa and since 400 AD or whenever the site was abandoned, the cinders had become buried deep in plants and soil.

Now the late coal seams (that is, seams dating from the Late Carboniferous period) that were probably used at the time were notorious for their impurities: sulphur, chlorine, phosphorous etc, and over the passage of time these noxious chemicals were probably released from the 'sunburnt' coal and gently mixed under the layers of soil and plants.

So those poor unsuspecting villagers must have dug into a reservoir of poison gas, possibly phosgene, which is one the gases they used in the First World War (and at the time we were at the party, the stuff Saddam was using on his people in Iraq).

So there you are, said my companion, "I don't need to visit do I?"

As a postscript there is somewhere a reference to a gold cup found in the cinders but it is said to have vanished without trace. Perhaps you should check your lofts?

Highwaymen and Hangman's Corner

Anthony and Doreen Jones

Nearly 40 years ago, my wife and I bought part of Cwm Oergwm from John Pugh, whose family had owned the entire east side of the valley for many years. John showed me a map of his property drawn on sheepskin, on which were marked the ruins of a building known as Highwayman's Cottage. The highwayman was reputed to ride across Cefn Cyff to reach the old coach road, known as the Gap Road, where he held up coaches and robbed the travellers.

Our two children were intrigued by this story and spent many hours on horseback trying to locate the Highwayman's Cottage. They eventually found its overgrown remains in a slight hollow in the Cwm Cwareli. My wife and I subsequently rode up to view the site.

We do not know any details of the highwayman's demise but we understand that the junction of the road past Tŷ Mawr farm and the Talybont road has been known in the past as Hangman's Corner. We wonder if there is any connection to the highwayman?

Pont y Caniedydd – The Singing Bridge

The completely rebuilt Pont y Caniedydd

Mary Jones (née Davies) Trosnant, Cantref, remembered warnings to be careful of going near Pont y Caniedydd, which spans the Nant Sere in the dip between Crofftau and Bailea, on the night of Hallowe'en, because this was a night when the old witch who lived in the water below might appear!

Translated, Pont y Caniedydd means the Singing Bridge, though no one knows why. Was it the witch who sang or was it the people who lived in the now vanished hamlet which once existed here? Maybe it was just named after the sound of the water in the Nant Sere, bubbling underneath. If there is a witch, her home was badly disturbed in 2005 when the bridge, being too weak to take heavy vehicles, was demolished and completely rebuilt by Powys County Council. No one knows if she has taken up residence again…

Welsh – Cymraeg

Welsh is one of the oldest languages in Europe. It has its roots in the Celtic language spoken in Britain around 600 BC, which then evolved as a language called Brythonic. From this descended Breton, Cornish and the Welsh we know today.

In the 19th century the language came under severe threat, because of a belief that English was superior, and was the only language that should be used throughout the British Empire.

The mid-19th century was a turbulent time in Wales. Life in the mines and working for the rich ironmasters in new industries of the South Wales Valleys often meant child labour, starvation wages and dangerous working conditions. English landowners taxed farmers for taking their crops to market by charging tolls on vital roads. Popular uprisings and riots, particularly the Rebecca Riots, broke out across the country. Questions were raised in Westminster as to why the Welsh people were prone to lawlessness.

A report of 1847, 'Brad y Llyfrau Gleision' – 'The Treason of the Blue Books', written by three English barristers who did not speak one word of Welsh between them, castigated Welsh culture in general, and Welsh schools in particular. They concluded that the Welsh language was a drawback and that the moral and material condition of the Welsh would only improve with the introduction of the English language.

Welsh Not Spoken

This period is associated with that most hated symbol of English cultural oppression, the Welsh Not, a means of forcing Welsh children to speak English at school. A stick or plaque was hung round the neck of any child heard speaking Welsh during school hours, to be handed on to whoever next spoke the language. At the end of lessons, the child left with the Welsh Not was beaten.

Leslie Williams grew up with the story of one of his forebears, "Revd Powell, born in Devynock (Defynnog) in 1788, who refused to give up speaking Welsh in school. He suffered the ignominy of having to wear the Welsh Not around his neck for speaking too much Welsh, punishment which caused him to cry bitterly." Leslie says Lewis Powell never forsook the Welsh language nor his Protestant faith.

The Language of Home and Heart

For Eirwen Stephens, Welsh was the language of home and Chapel. Her family farmed in the heart of the Welsh-speaking community of Penderyn and Hirwaun, so when she married Denzil Stephens and moved to Cantref, which was mainly English-speaking, she had to make a huge adjustment.

**Eirwen Stephens (née Davies) of Cantref, with her grandparents
Gwrthefyr and Eliza Roderick and her mother Amy Davies
At Berthlwyd Farm, Hirwaun**

"The Welsh language and Welsh Chapel and singing in Welsh I missed very much, as there were very few people who spoke Welsh in Cantref: only Mrs Tom Phillips (Bessie Bailea), Mr Richard Davies (Dick Tyle Llwyd), Mr David Davies and Mr Evan Evans of Upper Cantref. It was great to converse in Welsh to these people. But the kindness of the Cantref community shone through and I soon settled.

"It is marvellous that more people are learning and speaking Welsh these days. For me one of the best things that has happened is that our new Priest-in-Charge, Ven Randolph Thomas and his wife Jean are both Welsh speakers.

"To receive communion in my own language, for the first time in 50 years, was a deeply moving and important moment."

In fact Eirwen did more than settle down. She served the community as a Community Councillor, president of the Womens' Institute, hill farmer and friend to all. In particular she and her friend Glenys Pugh, who farmed at Plas y Gaer, Cantref with her late husband Ken, became a real team – the very best kind of wise, kind and pretty tough Welsh women farmers, who are a force to be reckoned with!

Photograph Susan Brook

Eirwen Stephens and her great friend Glenys Pugh

Today many newcomers to the area are enthusiastic about learning Welsh, the children all learn Welsh in school and some go to the Welsh medium School, Ysgol y Bannau, where all the lessons happen in Welsh.

Malcolm Llywelyn and his wife Jean, who live in Llanfrynach, do a huge amount to keep the Welsh language alive. Malcolm has run Welsh conversation evenings over a pint in the White Swan and writes for the Welsh-language community paper, 'Y Fan a'r Lle', (a phrase most aptly translated as 'On the Spot') which circulates in Brecon and the surrounding area and includes regular reports from Llanfrynach and Cantref.

It's always great to get an email from Malcolm. Not for him the usual Hi – but "Shwmae" and at the end "Hwyl!". And you get the same cheery Welsh greetings and a wave from him as he cycles round the village.

Cymraeg

Malcolm Llywelyn

Photograph Christine Cummins.

Shwmae! Jean and Malcolm Llywelyn with Willow

The 1891 Census of Population for Wales was the first census to include the status of the Welsh language. No separate figures were available for Llanfrynach and Cantref, but the census for Brecon records that the number of residents who spoke Welsh was 53.4%. The County census for Breconshire recorded 37.8% of residents speaking Welsh. Spoken Welsh declined from 54.5% of the population of Wales in the 1891 census to its lowest, 18.6%, in 1991; however, an increase to 20.52% was recorded in the 2001 census. The census for the Llanfrynach Community Council records the number of residents over the age of three who spoke Welsh was 61 out of 560 or 10.89%. The number of residents who declared some knowledge of Welsh was 41, or 7.32%.

The 1891 census was the last occasion when Welsh was the dominant language over English. Kim Brook, Cantref, describes himself as one of the 'gap generation'. His mother's first language was Welsh, but like many of her generation thought that to get on in the world her children should speak English. Leslie Williams chose to learn French at the local grammar school but, like Kim and many of his generation, in later life he regretted not learning Welsh.

However, there has been a significant increase in the use of the Welsh language in recent times and the language is still heard in Llanfrynach and Cantref. An increasing number of children from the area attend the Ysgol Meithrin (Nursery school) and the Welsh-language primary school at Ysgol y Bannau in Brecon, and will progress to the Welsh Stream at the High School. Older people who missed out on a Welsh education and newcomers to the country are learning the language and today it is seen as a real advantage both professionally and socially.

Where We Belong – The Place-Names

Malcolm Llywelyn

It is significant that so many place-names in Llanfrynach and Cantref are in Welsh and this probably reflects the status and prevalence of the language in the past. The following list is an attempt to translate or explain the meaning of these delightful names of farms, houses and places in our community. The names are in alphabetical order with translations in italics followed by some information on meaning or historical significance.

Abercynrig: *Mouth of Cynrig.* The River Cynrig joins the Usk below Abercynrig House. Abercynrig was granted to Sir Reginald Awbrey, as a reward for his support, by Bernard of Neufmarche in the 11th century. Bernard of Neufmarche was the Norman lord who built the castle in Brecon in 1093. Abercynrig was purchased by Mr John Lloyd of Dinas near Llanwrtyd in the 18th century and the house at Abercynrig was built by his son, who named it 'Dinas' after his ancestral home.

Afon Cynrig: *River from highest point.* Cynrig derives from 'cyn' meaning head, chief or highest point, 'rhig' is a stream or current from the latin 'rigo', which means to flow, a brook. Cynrig is also derived from the personal noun Cynwrig or Cynfrig, which was anglicised to the modern surname Kendrick. The source of the Cynrig is Nant Sere in Cwm Sere below Pen y Fan – the highest point.

Bailea: *Farmyards or enclosures.* Plural of beili.

Bailyhelig: *Enclosure of willow trees.* It is said that farms with the name 'beili' are on or were old fortified sites.

Bannau Brycheiniog: *Peaks or mountains of the land of Brychan.* Brychan Brycheiniog was the fifth century ruler of Breconshire. Many of the sons and daughters of Brychan became saints, to whom many churches throughout Wales have been dedicated.

Berllan: *Orchard.*

Brynteg: *Fairhill.*

Cae Caradog: *Caradog's field.*

Caerau: *Strongholds or enclosures.* It can also mean the plural of forts or walls.

Cantref Church: Originally dedicated to St. Cynidr, a 6th century saint and a grandson of Brychan Brycheiniog. The festival of St. Cynidr is said to have been celebrated on the 8th December. Cantref Church was re-dedicated to St. Mary in Norman times, but Cynidr has recently been restored and included in a joint dedication.

Cantref: *Hundreds: hundred homesteads or settlements.* An old administrative unit. In pre-Norman times, in accordance with tradition, old Brycheiniog was divided between the three sons of the ancient ruler of the area, Einon ap Gruffudd ab Elis, namely Selyf, Tewdos and Einon. Thus we had Cantref Selyf in the north and Cantref Tewdos or Cantref Mawr, which lay South of the river Usk and included the Bannau Brycheiniog; and Cantref Einon centred on Talgarth. (ap/ab means *son of* in Welsh.)

Capel Twyn: *Chapel on the hill.* A place of worship from 1864 to 1958. A branch of the Plough Chapel in Brecon. *(see also Mynydd Fernach: Brynach's Mountain.)*

Cefn Cantref: *Ridge of Cantref.*

Cefn Cyff: *Coffin Ridge.*

Cefn Meri: *Ridge of 'Meri'.*

Coed Cae'r ebol: *Colt's field wood.*

Coed Tyle Du: *Wood of the black hill.*

Coed y Brenin: *The king's wood.* Another site of a smaller Iron Age fort.

Coed y Caerau: *Wood of the enclosures.* The site of a large Iron Age fort.

Corn Du: *Black pointed peak or stack.*

Cribyn: *Ridge of hill or little crest.*

Crofftau: *Crofts or small enclosed fields.*

Cwm Cwareli: *Quarry valley.*

Cwm Cynwyn: *Head of white Valley.* *(According to local knowledge Cwm Cynwyn is also known as 'Valley of the early lambs'.)*

Cwm Gwdi: *Valley of the Gwdi stream.* It is understood 'gwdi' was the old name of a local stream. Maybe it could also be derived from 'gwdihw'. which is one of the Welsh words for owl, the other word is tylluan. *(Owl's valley!)*

Cwm Oergwm Isaf: *Lower cold valley.* The location of the Brecknock Wildlife Nature Reserve.

Cwm Oergwm: *Cold valley.*

Cwm Sere: *'Sere' valley.*

Fan y Big: *Tapered peak.*

Felindre: *Mill cottage or mill settlement.*

Glanusk: *Bank of the Usk*, a corruption of the Welsh 'Wysg'.

Homlas: *Hom? (g)las – blue or green.* (The g in glas disappears in a soft mutation.)

Llanbrynean: *Hillhouse.* A 19th century house built by David Morgan, the founder of the David Morgan Store in Cardiff, which closed in 2005. Llan originally referred to a house or building enclosed by a defensive hedge or wall. It more commonly appears before the name of a saint as the name of a church and a parish or village.

Llanfrynach: *Church of Saint Brynach.* The church is dedicated to the 5th century Celtic Saint of Irish origin.

Llwyn y fron: *Hillside.*

Llwyncelyn: *Hollybush.* Llwyn can also mean grove.

Llwyncynydd: *Grove of the master of hounds.*

Maesderwen: *Field of oak tree.* The house was built early in the 19th century. The remains of a Roman villa nearby were discovered in 1783, which may have been built in the third century during the reign of the 'Gallic' Emperors. In a field on the estate, called 'Cae Croff', according to legend, treasure is concealed and anyone attempting to dig it up would be frightened by apparitions and some would be 'running mad' and others 'lamed'. (See pages 196 and 197.)

Mizpah: Baptist Chapel from 1863 to 1970.

Mynydd Fernach: *Brynach's Mountain.* Bernach is the Irish for Brynach. Theophilus Jones refers to Mynydd Fernach in his 'History of Breconshire', although there is no record of it on recent maps. Deeds held by Sue and Graham Chamberlain of Capel Twyn indicate that their property is situated in the area of Mynydd Fernach.

Nant Cynwyn: *Head of white stream.*

Nant Menascin: *Stream flowing to the Usk.* Theophilus Jones in his 'History of Breconshire', claims 'me' in Welsh, similar to 'meo' in Latin, means to flow, signifies a liquid. He maintains 'hascin' is a corruption of 'wyscin', a sreamlet, the diminutive of 'wy' or 'wysk', the latter probably derives from Wysg, the Welsh word for Usk. The source of Nant Menascin is from Cwm Oergwm below Fan y Big and it joins the Usk near Pencelli: *Grovesend.*

Nant Sere: *'Sere' stream.*

Neuadd: *Hall or mansion.* A 16th century house.

Pannau: *Falling field or hollow.* Described as a 17th century house.

Pant: *Hollow.*

Pen y Fan: *Top of the ridge or peak.*

Pen yr Heol: *Top of the Road.*

Pencaefadog: *Top of Madog's field.* The name Madog, anglicised to Maddocks, may refer to the Madoc family of Llanfrynach, dating back to the 17th century. Thomas ap John Madoc was a descendant of Bleddyn ap Meinarch, the last Prince of Powys.

Pentwyn: *Top of the hill, top of the slope.*

Plas y Gaer: *Hall of the fortress or stronghold.* A late 17th century house and may refer to the site of an ancient fort or stronghold. Plas can also mean mansion and open space from an old Welsh word. Plas y Gaer was the site of the largest Iron Age fort in Brycheiniog sometime during the first four centuries before the birth of Christ. It is thought that such forts were built on mountain slopes to keep cattle, goats and some sheep safe from thieves and wild beasts!

Pont y Caniedydd or Pont Caniedydd; *Cynidr or Cynedd Bridge.* It was known as Pont Kenneddyr in 1670 and Pont Cyneddyd in 1711. Caniedydd probably originates from Cynedd, Kenedr and Cynidr and it is possibly a corrupted form of Pont Cynidr. *'Bridge of the songster'* is a lyrical translation and it has also been described as the *Singing Bridge'*, from the song of the stream, Nant Sere, which flows beneath.

Pontbrengarreg: *Wooden bridge of the stone.* Described as a late 16th century gentleman's house built before the Civil War.

Rhiwiau: *Hills or slopes.* This was also the site of a smaller Iron Age fort.

The Held: *Wood or holding.* Held is an old English word for 'slope', which often occurs in the Border Counties as a wood held with the manor. Hence the 'Held Wood' between Cantref and Ffrwdgrech. Held is also said to be a translation of the Welsh word gafael which meant a share of land inherited by sons from their father's land.

Tir Ciw: *Land or ground for shoeing cattle.* Ciw is a special kind of shoe made for cattle.

Tir Hir: *Long land.*

Tir y Groes: *Land of the Cross.*

Tregaer: *Farm or homestead of the fort or fortified place.* Tre(f) originally meant a large farm or land surrounding a dwelling after the clearing of a forest. The contemporary meaning of 'Tre' is a town.

Trosnant: *Scattered stream.*

Twyn: *Hill or slope.*

Tŷ Fry: *Upper house.* A 17th century house, once the home of William Phillips, the Recorder of Brecon between 1689 and 1707. A room in the house was used as a school room before the village school was built in 1853.

Tŷ Mawr: *Grand house.* A Victorian-gothic house.

Tyle Llwyd: *Brown Hill.* Tyle can mean hill or ascent and llwyd also means holy, grey or brown.

Tylebrythos: *Brindled hill.* Brythos may be derived from brith which means brindled.

Tynllwyn: *Grove house.* A field nearby, 'cae gwin' which is probably derived from "carn gwyn", meaning, *white mound of stones.* A cistfaen – *a stone coffin,* was found in 1808. The remains of human bones and a fragment of a skull were found in the coffin, considered to be the interment of a British chieftain from the early ages of Christianity.

Waunberllan: *Orchard meadow.*

Wern y Fran: *Meadow of crows.*

Wern y Marchog: *Rider's meadow.* Marchog can also mean knight. Hill shepherds on horseback have been described as 'marchogion y mynydd' – knights of the mountain.

Wern: *Alder trees or meadow.* Gwern, (g) disappears in mutation

Wernddu: *Black meadow.*

Wysg: *Usk.* Wysg is derived from the Latin word isca, which meant fish. It is believed to have been the headquarters of the Roman Second Legion. 'Isca Augusta' was the fort 'Gobannio' in Abergavenny on the banks of the Usk and this is how the name of the river originated.

Ysgubor Newydd: *New Barn.*

References:

The Welsh Language and the 1891 Census: Gwenfair Parry & Mari A. Williams.
Welsh Place Names of Breconshire: Dewi Davies.
Some Breconshire Place-Names: Brycheiniog, Vol. 11 1965: Stephen J. Williams.
A Study of Breconshire Place-Names: Richard Morgan & R.F. Peter Powell.
History of Breconshire: Theophilus Jones.
Y Llyfr Enwau: D. Geraint Lewis.
2001 Census of Population, Key Statistics for Wales, Powys and Llanfrynach Community Council.
Atlas Brycheiniog: Pwyllgor Addysg Brycheiniog 1958/59.
Enwau Tir a Gwlad: Melville Richards

Source Material and Further Reading

Where We Belong – Ein Cynefin (first edition 2000)   Edited by Susan Brook
The Guiding Light
         Brecknockshire Agricultural Society 1755 - 2005   Leslie Williams
Flowing Tides Thomas Conway Lloyd (1905 – 1939)   John Sainsbury Caple
         (available online at 'Internet Archive,' no charge)
Traditional Industries of Rural Wales
         Self-Sufficiency to Dependency in the County of Brecon   Dr. Elwyn Bowen
Life in Llanfryach – the 1891 Census   Hilda Davies
The Drovers (pamphlet)   Brecknock Museum & Art Gallery
The Welsh Cattle Drovers   Richard J. Colyer
         University of Wales Press 1976
The Drovers   K.J. Bonser
         Robert Maclehose & Co. Ltd., University Press, Glasgow.
The Journal of Mary Gwladys Charles 1897 – 1903
         A Social History   Dr. A. Gareth Jones
People Power - The Human Stories behind South Wales'
         Industrial Heritage   Ruth Waycott, Herian.
The Seventeenth Century History of Brecknock   Rev. Jones Davies
Llanfrynach Church History   R.J.M. Sinnett
Church of SS Peter & Illtyd, Llanhamlach
(in Llanhamlach church)   David Morgan
Rags to Riches: Entrepreneurs of Welsh Origin   Jonathan Morgan

Our Farming Calendar

Photograph Garfield Kennedy

Calendar Boy

January:
The pregnant hill sheep are safely down from the hills. Shy wild mountain ponies come down to graze and the first lambs are born to the lowland sheep. Calving begins.

February:
The slopes of the old Rectory garden behind Cantref Church are carpeted with snowdrops. Lambing of the lowland sheep gets into full swing. On the hill farms where conditions are harsher, the lambs arrive later. All the sheep are on winter feed.

March:
St. David's Day festivities are enjoyed and hill sheep start lambing. Visitors arrive to enjoy pony trekking, walking and other outdoor activities. Volunteers maintain footpaths to fight the erosion caused by so many feet going to the top of the Beacons.

April:
Even in the high-tech 21st century lambing is much the same as it has always been – an exhausting round-the-clock job

May:
Cattle are turned out into the fields. Traditionally this gave farm workers time for the May Fair – to be hired for a new job or to have a much deserved break.

June:
Once again the sheep and lambs are gathered from the hills, sheared and sent back. Higher up the Beacons, where the temperature is always a couple of degrees cooler, there are bluebells and May blossom in flower.

July:
This is the time to harvest hay (which is dry) and silage (which is green) to store for winter feed.

August:
Brecon Jazz Festival and Brecon Agricultural Show attract thousands of people into the town and surrounding countryside. Meanwhile the sheep are brought down from the hills for dipping and the lambs are separated from their mothers.

September:
Ram sales are held locally and some farmers go further afield to Lockerbie in Scotland to one of the largest ram sales in the country. Each farm has to ensure it has new rams to "tup" the ewes.

October:
The sheep are brought off the hill again this time for winter dipping and for the beginning of the breeding year. Sheep are pregnant for five months and farmers decide when they want their flock to lamb.

November:
After another traditional farming holiday, the November Fair, the cattle are brought into sheds for the winter. They are not allowed in the fields during the winter because of the mess and the mud they create, not only undesirable but against EEC farming regulations. In fact these days the whole farming year involves a huge amount of paperwork to ensure all livestock is traceable and healthy.

December:
Time to scan the sheep – with a mobile ultra sound scanner to discover which are having singles, twins or maybe even triplets. The fat stock show (animals ready for killing) and the poultry sale are held. Finally there is the feathering of turkeys, geese and poultry for Christmas.

Cantref

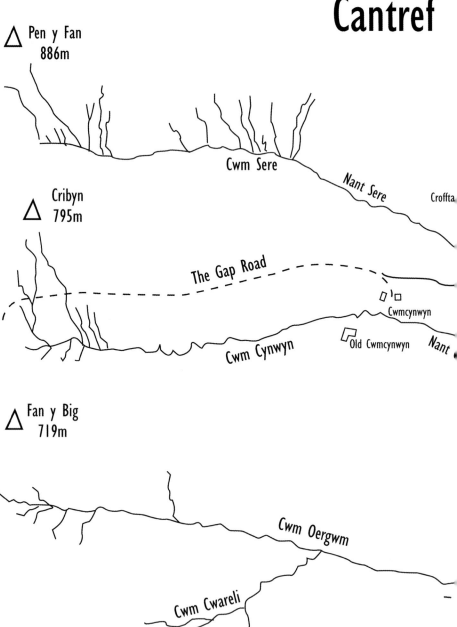

△ Pen y Fan
886m

Cwm Sere

Nant Sere

Croffta

△ Cribyn
795m

The Gap Road

Cwmcynwyn

Old Cwmcynwyn

Nant

Cwm Cynwyn

△ Fan y Big
719m

Cwm Oergwm

Cwm Cwareli

anfrynach

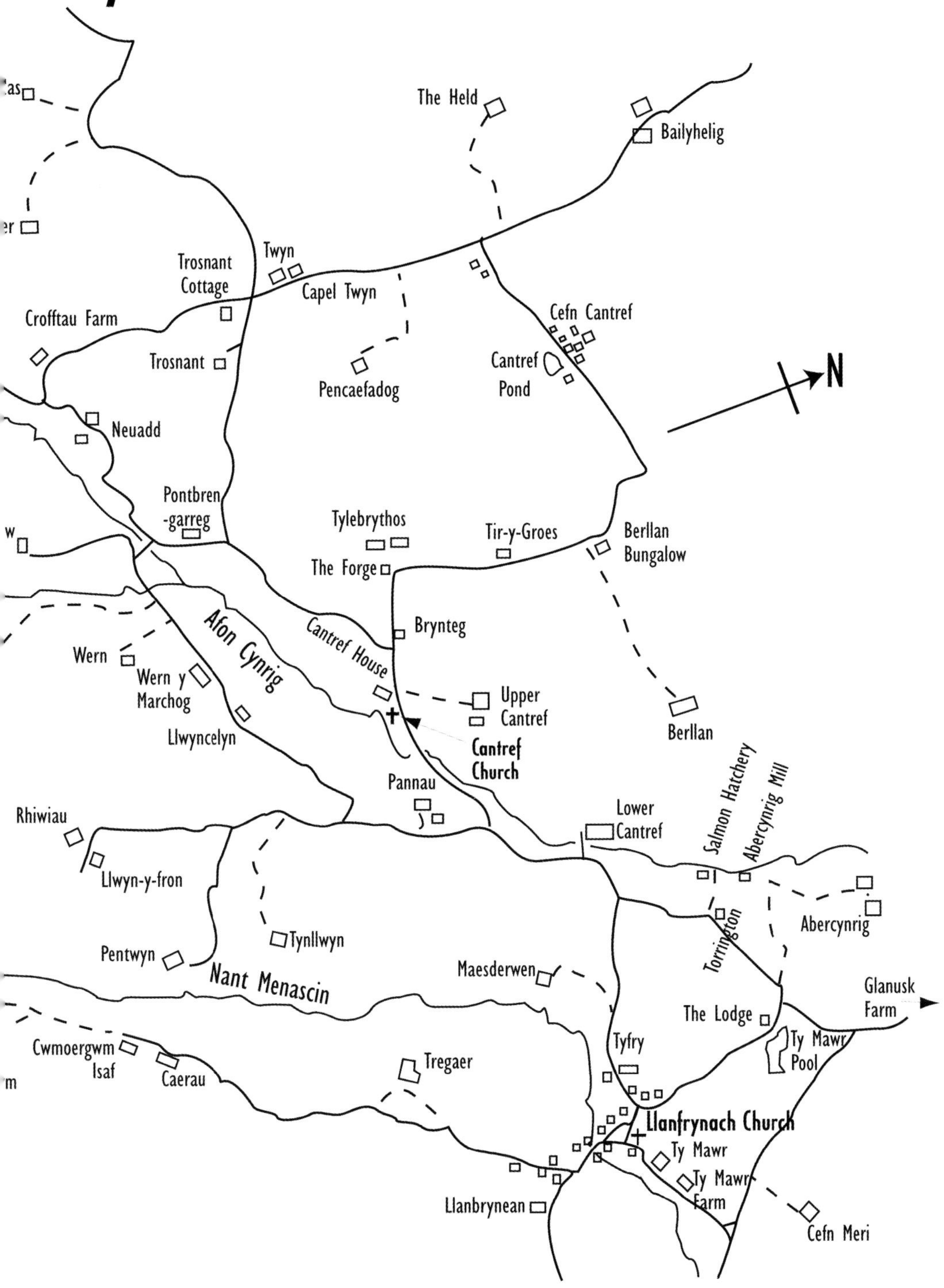

The Held

Bailyhelig

Cas

er

Twyn

Trosnant
Cottage

Capel Twyn

Cefn Cantref

Crofftau Farm

Trosnant

Cantref
Pond

Pencaefadog

N

Neuadd

Pontbren
-garreg

Tylebrythos

Tir-y-Groes

Berllan
Bungalow

w

The Forge

Brynteg

Cantref House

Wern

Wern y
Marchog

Afon Cynrig

Upper
Cantref

Berllan

Llwyncelyn

Cantref
Church

Pannau

Rhiwiau

Lower
Cantref

Salmon Hatchery

Abercynrig Mill

Llwyn-y-fron

Abercynrig

Torrington

Pentwyn

Tynllwyn

Nant Menascin

Maesderwen

Glanusk
Farm

The Lodge

Ty Mawr
Pool

Cwmoergwm
Isaf

Caerau

Tregaer

Tyfry

m

Llanfrynach Church

Ty Mawr

Ty Mawr
Farm

Llanbrynean

Cefn Meri